JOHN • LESLIE

AGING MEMORY

MAKE YOUR AGING MEMORY SHARP AS A TACK!

All rights reserved. No part of this book may be reproduced, stored, or transmitted by any means—whether auditory, graphic, mechanical, or electronic—without written permission of both publisher and author, except in the case of brief excerpts used in critical articles and reviews. Unauthorized reproduction of any part of this work is illegal and is punishable by law.

ISBN 978-0-6922-9724-7
Printed in The United States of America
First Printing October 2014

Little Red Hen Book Group
Spring, Texas

ABOUT THE AUTHOR

John Leslie continues to explore the role of seniors in their response to contemporary moral issues. This book addresses one of the biggest problems of older citizens: "As I age, how can I continue to be mentally alert and responsive? What help can I be to a society that praises and rewards those younger and tends to ignore the aging?"

This fifth book in his series contains straight-forward and easy-to-follow memory enabling rules. It is a response to the mature quest to remember yesterday's and today's events.

It is his belief that aging citizens are the cornerstone of the future, but they must earn the right to express their views on contemporary issues by demonstrating mental acuity. A mind that remembers is an important part of evaluating and understanding the past and developing intelligent responses to the future.

John and his wife, Janice, reside in Houston, Texas.

*"What we think, or what we know, or what we believe is, in the end, of little consequence.
The only consequence is what we do."*
John Ruskin

DEDICATION

This book is for every senior who has wondered, "Where is that?" or "When did that happen?" or "What's his name?" or "What was I looking for?"

At one time or another, we've forgotten…and as we age we worry about "losing it" permanently. It may not help to know that civilizations have been having memory problems forever! The Bible mentions it. Ecclesiastes 1: 2-11 says, "Nobody remembers what happened yesterday. And the things that will happen tomorrow? Nobody will remember them either. Don't count on being remembered."

However, good teacher that it is, the Bible tells us there's a way to do better and offers some advice: use our heads. From Ecclesiastes 10:10, "Remember: The duller the ax, the harder the work. Use your head; the more brains, the less muscle." This book exemplifies that theme.

The Bible addresses the value of using the teachings of others so that learning about remembering will be easier. 1 Corinthians 4:17 says, "This is why I sent Timothy to you earlier. He is also my dear son, and true to the Master. He will refresh your memory on the instructions I regularly give all the churches on the way of Christ."

Professionals use many techniques to remember. You can use them too. The ones I believe most helpful to seniors are described in this book. But there are other ways, some of which are described in the addendums. This book's emphasis is on ways to enable seniors to gain self-confidence by learning ways to stay "sharp."

There is a way—an easy way—to recall anything you want to. The way…the answers…are within the pages of this book.

Scriptural references are based on Eugene Peterson's book, "The "Message," the Bible in contemporary language.

CHAPTERS

xii   Important Information That Will Start You On Your Journey

PART 1 -- GETTING STARTED

1   Your Mind 2
2   Your Aging Memory.. 3
3   Why Can't I Remember? 12
4   The Seven Sins of Memory 29
5   Memory Myths 32

PART 2 -- YOU CAN DO IT!

6   The Best is Yet to Come 40
7   Are You Just Intelligent or Are You a Genius? 44
8   You Have the Power! 49
9   Why You Don't Remember 54
10   Fun With Memory 62

PART 3 -- DO IT!

11   Memory Techniques Vocabulary 86
12   Survey, Question, Read, Recite, Review 92
13   Mnemonics 95
14   Building Memory Skills: A Quick Preview 107
15   The Phonetic Alphabet 109
16   Remember Every Number 112
17   Visualization and Association 120
18   The Consonant Peg System 125
19   Chunking 136
20   Linking 140

21	The Memory Palace	145
22	Remember Names and Faces	152
23	Remember Word for Word	165
24	Remember a Script	170
25	Remember Phone Numbers	173
26	Remember License Numbers	176
27	In Conclusion	178

ADDENDUM

1	Other Peg Systems	181
2	Practical Strategies for Remembering	188
3	Memory Books	190
4	Don't Want to Learn any Memory Techniques?	193
5	More Great Easy Ways to Enhance Your Everyday Memory	199
6	A Memory Palace Journey	217
7	Characteristics of Memory	223

IMPORTANT INFORMATION TO START YOU ON YOUR JOURNEY

All learning is based on memory. All memory is based on the association of one thing to another.

Creating a memory event connects one thing to another: a name to a face, a phone number or an address to a person or company, or the definition or meaning of a word, or an event to a happening.

The basic rule of memory is that you can remember any new piece of information if it is intentionally associated in some way to something you already know. Easy-to-learn memory techniques will enable you to create images and consciously associate the image of what you want to remember to an image of something you already know. Once the techniques are habits, you'll have a trained memory, and all learning will be easier for you the rest of your life.

It is effortless to remember things that have meaning and can be pictured (these are tangible images). It is not easy to remember or picture intangible things. So, substitute tangible images for intangibles (picture one item instead of the other). It also helps to make the image out of proportion (imagine the item as larger than life), or exaggerate (see millions instead of one).

Our minds capture information and store it in our minds. Harry Lorayne, a giant in memory techniques, called it "Original Awareness." Nothing you are originally aware of can be forgotten. However, unless there is a way to recall it, the stored information is worthless. Learn how to recall stored information by using one of the many techniques described in this book.

MAKE YOUR AGING MEMORY SHARP AS A TACK

NOTE: This book is primarily my personalization of work done by others, modified (in some instances), and enlarged (where additional clarification was needed), and shortened (in others), along with my observations. My contribution was collecting what I thought would be of most value to seniors. I have edited, clarified, and supplemented almost everything. Whenever the contribution of another person is clear, I've given them credit.

If the techniques are beneficial to you, my editing and small original contributions were successful. If you don't use any of the ideas...the work of others...and mine, then this book was not helpful. I hope that is not the case.

PART 1
Getting Started

An important part of memory involves decisions you make.

It's possible your memories are handicapped by your past. The chapters in this section are intended to expand your understanding of the ways your mind functions in different situations.

Your memory skills will increase as you are equipped to evaluate why your mind does some of the things it does. This section sets the stage for the development of a superior memory.

If this kind of background material is not your thing, skip to Part 3.

CHAPTER 1
YOUR MIND

How would you like someone to say these things to you?

I am on your side.

Everything that occurs between us is confidential.

If anyone is told about what occurs between us, it will be you.

I am available to you in any situation; just ask.

I am the teacher; you are the learner.

Don't argue with me. Remember, I am the teacher, you are the learner, and your lack of knowledge need not embarrass you. Remember our confidentiality agreement.

I know things you have forgotten.

I will help you recall information you thought you had forgotten.

I will help you combine ideas and thoughts in ways that are amazing.

I need exercise, just as you do. We can do it alone or together.

Neither of us is ever too old to change, to learn, to explore.

Your past is mine forever; I'll help you remember it. The future is ours; we share it.

We can imagine, analyze, develop, change, erase, improve, alter, create, verbalize, write—there is no limit to what you and I are capable of doing…as long as you remember we are nothing without each other.

I am your mind.

CHAPTER 2
YOUR AGING MEMORY

Everyone has trouble remembering some things. Below is a list (it's not complete) of things that are memory challenges to some of us.

Actors and their pictures	Names
Authors	Names of songs
Birthdays	Numbers
Book names/authors/plots	Paintings/artists
Characters in a book, play or movie	Passwords
	Portrait names
Combinations safe/locks	Phone numbers
Dates	Playing cards
Directions	Plots of pictures or books
Dramatic productions	Political data
Faces	Presentations
Facts and figures	Recent events
Hiding places for objects	Recipes
Jokes	Room arrangements
License plates	Scriptures
Lists	Speech content
Location of objects	Stocks and bonds
Medications	Story plots
Medicare number	Telephone numbers
Meetings	TV shows/schedules
Movies/movie stars	The "Arts"

The list could go on and on. Every one of us forgets.

If you have trouble remembering any of the topics on this list, take heart! Remembering some"thing" is difficult for most of us.

But there's a way to remember everything! And, better yet, the way to a better memory is easy...regardless of your age.

If asked, how would you think you would do in a memory functions test? Responding with a "guess" or an "estimate" is not a measurable response. The guys in the white coats say an estimate is a "subjective memory" response. Subjective memory is perception. It cannot be scored.

But if given a pen and paper memory test which can be scored, you'd find out how you really did. There would be a score. This is the way objective memory is identified. It can be measured.

There are two things to remember so far: subjective memory and objective memory. Objective memory counts.

There has always been a question of who is better at remembering things, men or women? Scientists tell us memory and other cognitive skills often vary according to gender:

    Women tend to have better verbal and language abilities.

    Men have the edge in spatial and mathematical abilities.

Believe it or not. But there is no doubt memory skills change if nothing is done to keep them up to speed. In all likelihood, your memory has changed as you've aged. Change in memory ability is a phenomenon called "age-associated memory impairment."

    40% of us are affected by this condition in our fifties, 50% in our sixties, and 70% in our seventies.

CHAPTER 2 YOUR AGING MEMORY

Changes in our brains, along with memory difficulties, are part of a continuous, fluid process that began early in our lives. **You will learn how to keep your memory sharp for a long, long time.**

Here's a short objective memory test. (Remember? Objective memory is the kind of memory that can be measured.) Study the following words for a minute.

Plank
Banker
Sauce
Umbrella
Abdomen
Reptile
Lobster
Orchestra
Forehead
Jury

We'll come back to the list in a minute to test your recall, but for now, do you know these facts?

The USA population in 2010 was 308,745,538. In 2000, it was 281,424,602.

In 2010, 40 million people 65 and over lived in the United States, accounting for 13 percent of the total population. The older population grew from 3 million in 1900 to 40 million in 2010.

The oldest-old population (those 85 and over) grew from just over 100,000 in 1900 to 5.5 million in 2010.

The "Baby Boomers" (those born between 1946 and 1964) started turning 65 in 2011. As a result, the number of older people will increase dramatically during the 2010–2030 period. The older population in 2030 is projected to be twice as large as their counterparts in 2000, growing from 35 million to 72 million and representing nearly 20 percent of the total U.S. population.

The Census Bureau projects that the 85-year olds and older population could grow from 5.5 million in 2010 to 19 million by 2050. Some researchers predict that death rates for oldsters will decline more rapidly than is reflected in the Census Bureau's projections. If true, this older population will grow even faster.

By 2012, 100 million Americans were 50 years old or older. Increased life expectancies and energetic life styles have added 20 to 25% to a lifetime. In all probability, the additional years will be spent in retirement. (Franklin Roosevelt would never have thought it!)

As a starter for memory improvement, answer these questions (don't look back!):

What was the population of the US in 2010?

At the end of 2012, how many of us were 50 years old or older?

Of the word list from the previous page, how many of the 10 can you recall? Write them down.

Now look back. Your score:

CHAPTER 2 YOUR AGING MEMORY

8 or grearter	
4 to 7	
less than 4	

There's a neat way to remember lists like this: Make a story of the words by linking the words together into a ridiculous story. For example:

> The **banker** stepped out of the **orchestra** onto the **plank** before the **jury.** Opening his **umbrella,** a **lobster** and a **reptile** fell out, striking his **forehead** and bouncing off his **abdomen**. "Hum," he thought to himself, "a little **sauce** would make both a good meal."

If you'd put the words together in a similar way, the confusing facts and figures you heard right after looking at the list wouldn't matter.

The memory technique you've demonstrated is called "Linking." More about linking later; for now, move on.

Let's try another list, our second objective memory test. Make a story of the following words:

Ink	Monarch
Kettle	Steamer
Spray	Dirt
Musician	Lawn
Volcano	Gallery

What was your story? Here are some possibilities:

> When the **volcano** erupted, the **ink** in the **kettle spray(ed)** over the **musician.** Luckily, the **Monarch's** throne was on the **steamer**, but **dirt** from the **lawn** flew onto the **gallery.**

Here's another one:

> The **ink** was boiling in the **kettle**. The **spray** flew onto the **musician** as he was staring at the **volcano** and the **Monarch's steamer.** He watched as **dirt** from the **lawn** blew into the **gallery**.

And another:

> The **Monarch** and the **musician** heard the **volcano** from the deck of the **steamer. Dirt** from the **gallery**, as well as pieces of **lawn**, fell into the **kettle** of **ink** and **sprayed** over everyone.

Getting back to the list, how many of the 10 words can you recite from memory?

Your score:

	This test	First test
8 or greater		
4 to 7		
less than 4		

You probably did better on the second test. Remembering lists is not easy, but there are ways to make remembering unconnected things a lot easier than staring at them and hoping

CHAPTER 2 YOUR AGING MEMORY

you'll remember. **Linking** (which you've just experienced) is one memory technique that can be used to remember lists.

How often do these topics present a memory problem to you? Respond either "always," "sometimes," or "never."

- Names
- Faces
- Appointments
- Where I put things (e.g., keys, eyeglasses)
- List of household chores
- Directions to places
- Phone numbers just looked up
- Phone numbers used frequently
- Things people tell me
- Correspondence responses
- Personal dates (e.g., birthdays)
- Words
- What I wanted to buy at the store
- Taking a test
- Beginning something and forgetting what you were doing
- Losing the thread of thought in conversation
- Losing the sequence of thoughts when speaking in public
- Knowing whether you have already told someone something

As you read a novel do you have trouble remembering:
- The opening chapters, after you've finished the book?
- Three or four chapters before the one now being read?
- Chapter before the one now being read?
- Paragraph just before the one now being read?
- Sentence just before the one now being read?

How well do you remember things that occurred:

Yesterday?
Last week?
Last month?
Between six months and one year ago?
Between one and five years ago?

Are things getting better because we're living longer? It could be. "Old" doesn't mean what it used to. In fact, "old" has been redefined:

Young Old—65-74 years
Old—75-84
Old-old—85+

The "old—old segment of the population (those 85+years old) is the fastest growing, as already noted. The numbers in this population segment are twice those 65 and over. Representing about 10% of the total 2010 population, the ranks of the "old—old" will triple from the 5.5 million alive in 2010 to over 19 million by 2050.

Declining fertility and improved health and longevity have swelled the older population dramatically and at an unprecedented rate. Factors like these drive the increase in life expectancy:

Age Dynamics—past variations in birth and death rates (the period 1946 to 1964), created a lot of baby boomers!

Declining Fertility Rates—a declining share of younger people within the general population causes the population's share of older people to rise automatically.

Longevity—as the population ages, there is general agreement that the increase in life expectancy will continue. The 2012 newborn infant can expect to live for 78.3 years. Life expectancy at age 65 has increased more in the last 30 years than in the entire 200-year period from 1750 to 1950. Today, a man 75 years old has a 50/50 chance of reaching 84; a woman 86.

Gender—for every 100 women in the 65-74 age group, there are only 86 males. In the 75-84 age group, there are 72 males to every 100 women. In the 85 and older group, there are 49 men for every 100 women. However, men are living longer and women are dying earlier, so changes keep occurring.

Information like this is important because seniors want to be aware of what's happening as they age. Oldsters want to remember life's experiences, and, more importantly, they want to continue contributing.

CHAPTER 3
WHY CAN'T I REMEMBER?

What is the point of memorizing a string of numbers or the sequence of cards in a deck?

What is the point of a group of men running around a circular track as fast as they can?

What is the point of 11 football players batting heads against another group of 11?

All share wanting to succeed at what they're doing.

The good news is that you are able to improve your brain, just as an athlete trains his muscles and skills for his sport. You can succeed at this task.

This chapter explains some of the thinking traps that affect memory making (academically called "cognitive biases"). We may not be aware our understanding of reality may be flawed, or that our recall or deductive processes are not performing well. But these are correctble issues that cause us memory concerns.

Bias is a primary culprit. Without our agreement, it sets traps for us that can seriously hinder our ability to think rationally. However, bias is not the only troublemaker; there are many, many other cognitive issues. This chapter describes 10 of the most bothersome ones, but the list barely scratches the surface when illustrating how our thinking can be led askew. Wikipedia's list of cognitive biases includes more than 100 of these traps.

We are victims. We fall into the trap our mind sets for us. As a result, we sometimes make unwise decisions and/or reason improperly

CHAPTER 3 WHY CAN'T I REMEMBER?

Our minds, usually dependable and helpful, may get us into trouble. We can't use the "traps" for an excuse, but knowing about them should be helpful.

Here are 10 of the most harmful thinking traps:

Anchoring: Over-Relying on First Thoughts
Status Quo: Keep On Keeping On
Sunk Costs: Protecting Earlier Choices
Confirmation: Seeing What You Want to See
Incomplete Information: Review Your Assumptions
Conformity: Everybody Else is Doing It
Illusion of Control: Shooting in the Dark
Coincidence: We Suck at Probabilities
Recall: Not All Memories Are Created Equal
Superiority: The Average is Above Average

Here are explanations of the 10 memory traps:

1. Anchoring: Over-Relying on First Thoughts

"Is the population of Turkey greater than 35 million? What's your best estimate?"

Researchers asked this question to a group of people, and the estimates were seldom too far off 35 million. The same question was posed to a second group, but this time using 100 million as the starting point. Although both figures were arbitrary, the population estimates from the 100 million-group were higher than those in the 35 million group. (For the curious, according to a 2012 estimate, there are over 74 million people living in Turkey.)

Initial impressions, ideas, estimates, or data "anchor" subsequent thoughts. This impact on the cognitive starting point can heavily bias our thinking. This bias is particularly dangerous because it is deliberately used for many occasions. For example, experienced salespersons will show you a higher-priced item first, "anchoring" that price in your mind. Don't assume your first thoughts point to the correct answer.

What to do:

Always view a problem from different perspectives. Avoid being stuck with a single starting point.

Work on your problem statement before going down a solution path.

Think on your own before consulting others. Get as much data as possible and explore some conclusions by yourself before being influenced by other people's anchors.

Seek information from a wide variety of sources. Get many opinions and broaden your frame of reference.

Avoid being limited to a single point of view.

2. Status Quo: Keep On Keeping On

In one experiment, a group of people was randomly given one of two gifts: half received a decorated mug; the other half a large Swiss chocolate bar. They were then told that they could effortlessly exchange one gift for the other. Logic tells us that about half of people would not get the gift they preferred and would exchange it. In fact, only 10% did!

The status quo automatically has an advantage over every other alternative. We tend to repeat established behaviors

CHAPTER 3 WHY CAN'T I REMEMBER?

unless given the right incentives to entice us to change them.

Do this:

Consider the status quo as just another alternative. Don't get caught in the 'current vs. others' mindset.

Ask yourself if you would choose your current situation if it weren't the status quo.

Know your objectives. Be explicit about them and evaluate them objectively.

Avoid exaggerating or switching costs. Costs frequently are not as bad as we tend to assume.

3. Sunk Costs: Protecting Earlier Choices

Sunk costs are costs that cannot be recovered. It's something you've already spent and won't get back, regardless of future outcomes. It's like that gym club membership you bought: whether you get its benefits or not, the money is gone and there's no way to get it back.

Suppose you pre-ordered a non-refundable ticket to a basketball game. However, on the night of the game, you simply don't feel like going. You're tired, there's a blizzard raging outside and the game will be televised. You regret the fact that you bought the ticket because, frankly, you would prefer to stay at home, light up your fireplace, and comfortably watch the game on TV. But the fact is you did buy the ticket — and it was quite expensive and hard to get.

The point **is the money is already gone, so now you are better off doing what pleases you best.** Unless you can sell the ticket, just forget about what you paid for it. You are better off using it to help fuel the fireplace while you comfortably enjoy the game on TV.

Easier said than done.

There are many psychological blocks in the way of simply discarding an expensive ticket. And if that holds true for a mere basketball game ticket, imagine how strong that effect is when it comes to, say, abandoning a long-time relationship in which you've invested so much time, but that isn't working anymore.

That's the sunk cost bias. It's what you may have heard as "throwing good money after bad," but it isn't just about money: any type of investment you make—time, money, effort… anything—is subject to this sunk cost thinking trap.

Are you a sunk cost bias victim? Persisting with bad decisions due to an irrational attachment to costs that cannot be recovered has become so common you can find examples just about anywhere. Big organizations and governments excel at it. (For example, a government that insists on continuing a war so the lives already spent "are not wasted.")

This mental trap permeates decision-making. It affects not only organizations, but it deeply affects each of us at a personal level, too.

Here are some examples:

Bad overall life decisions: What would you say about remaining in an unfulfilling job or career just because you "invested so much time in it"? Or persisting in a bad relationship just to "make all those years worth it?" These are the saddest cases of the sunk cost effect, since people can literally waste years—if not their whole lives—because of it.

Bad financial decisions: Do you know anyone who refused to sell something (maybe property or stocks) for a perfectly reasonable price just because they've already spent so much money in it? What about casino gamblers who simply won't quit, claiming they need to make the money they've already lost "worth it?"

Bad everyday decisions: You ordered too much food, but you eat it anyway despite being full. You keep useless clutter in your home, only because you paid for it. You watch a bad movie up to the end, only because you started watching it. The examples go on and on. The consequences for each of them may seem trivial, but we make these mistakes so often that they add up quickly.

Why do we fall into the "sunk costs" trap? How can we avoid the trap?

If dwelling on sunk costs is a bad idea, why do we do it? More importantly, how do we overcome this thinking trap? Here are the main reasons why we do it, along with ways to overcome each of them.

We want to make the investment worth our while.

This is the fundamental reasoning behind how we deal with sunk costs. We have a genuine interest in making our efforts worthwhile. We don't want to feel that we spent anything in vain—time, money…anything. However, even if we know deep inside that our approach is wrong, we still have trouble abandoning it.

Do this:

>**Cut your losses and move on!** We all expect to have a good return on our investments. It would be insane not to. Just make sure you're not remaining in a situation solely because you made the investment in the first place.

>You don't make a bad move any better by dwelling more on it **unless** you can effectively make something happen that changes the expected outcome. Immediately stop spending resources on a bad move—throwing good money after bad—and start spending these resources on another, well-thought-out project.

We fear failing and looking foolish. We live in a success-oriented culture. Cutting losses means admitting you made a mistake, if not in public, at least to yourself. Our egos will always stubbornly try to hold us to our commitments so we don't admit our imperfections. If you made a public commitment, you're even less likely to break it, as there will probably be a lot of explaining to do.

Do this:

>**Allow yourself to make mistakes.** Quickly admitting your mistakes is much more productive than entrenching yourself in a situation just to "save face." Be aware that quitting is not failing (actually, sometimes it's exactly the opposite).

CHAPTER 3 WHY CAN'T I REMEMBER?

Better yet, do like Socrates and think differently: **be proud of admitting your errors.** Change your attitude from hiding mistakes to actively exposing them. Look for them: the more, the merrier. You'll surely feel defenseless and uneasy at first, but once you get used to it, you'll feel invulnerable to harsh criticism. Moreover, instead of focusing on the sunk costs, take pride in having recognized the costs associated with sticking to the old approach.

We become attached to our commitments. After we decide to do something, we feel attached to what we committed to. The bigger the commitment, the harder it is to let go. Not only that, it's a human trait to be overconfident that every thing we set ourselves to do will pay off. We're biased when we evaluate the probability of success of already-made commitments. (This is known as an "overly optimistic probability bias".)

Do this:

> **Be aware of the natural bias to stay on your current course of action.** While considering other options, evaluate the status quo as just another option, rather than the front-runner. Also, try to detach yourself emotionally from your past decisions. Be especially careful depending on things that worked in the past; this is not a guarantee they'll work in your favor again.
>
> **Practice "zero-based thinking."** Forget about the past and consider this very moment as your "point-zero" in time: act like all you have is the present. Do this by pretending you just woke up with some sort of amnesia. Imagine yourself in

your current situation, but without any knowledge of how you got there. This way, it's much easier to focus on the current situation, instead of clinging to past decisions that would drag you down.

We lose sight of our underlying goals. Sometimes we become so preoccupied by how much time and effort we've put into something that we lose sight of its relevance in the greater scheme of things. We become attached to the means and forget about the ends.

Do this:

>**Always be mindful of long-term objectives.** Don't confuse any greater goal you want to achieve with the specific means of implementation you're attached to. Don't get caught up in justifying your current actions. Using the movie example, suppose your original goal was to have fun, so you rented a movie. If the movie turns out to be a bad one, don't forget that your goal was not to spend two hours watching a movie, but to have fun. So, turn it off and go have fun, somehow.

>**Let go of the past, move on.** This is not a recommendation that you become a quitter. The point is to be always aware of your current situation. If you decide to stick with your current approach, that's great. Do it consciously and for the right reasons.

>**You will not recover your lost time.** The greatest example of sunk costs is your time, which you will not be able to recover. All of your life, until now, is gone. You can't reclaim

that time. Stop clinging to the past and make the most of your life **right now.**

4. Confirmation: Seeing What You Want to See

You feel the stock market will be going down and that now may be a good time to sell your stock. Just to be reassured of your hunch, you call a friend who has just sold all her stock to find out her reasons.

Congratulations. You have just fallen into the **Confirmation Trap.** It is a way of looking for information that will most likely support your initial point of view—while conveniently avoiding information that challenges it.

The confirmation bias affects not only where you go to collect evidence, but also how you interpret the data. We are much less critical of arguments that support our initial ideas and more resistant to arguments against them. No matter how neutral we think we are when first tackling a decision, our brains always decide—intuitively—on an alternative right away, making us subject to this trap virtually at all times.

Do this:

> **Expose yourself to conflicting information.** Examine all evidence with equal rigor. Don't be soft on information which disclaims your original thoughts. Know whether you are searching for alternatives or looking for reassurance!
>
> **Get a devil's advocate.** Find someone you respect to argue against the decision you're contemplating making. If you can't find one, build the counter arguments yourself. Always

consider the other positions with an open mind (taking into account the other mind traps).

Don't ask leading questions. When asking for advice, ask neutral questions to avoid people merely confirming your biases. "What should I do with my stocks?" works better than "Should I sell my stocks today?"

5. Incomplete information: Review your assumptions

Harry is an introverted guy. We know that he is either a librarian or a salesman. Which one do you think he is? We may be tempted to think he's a librarian. Haven't we been conditioned to think of salesmen as having outgoing, if not pushy, personalities?

This reasoning may be dead wrong (or at least incomplete). This conclusion neglects the fact that salesmen outnumber librarians about 100 to 1. Before you even consider Harry's character traits, you should have assigned only a 1% chance that he's a librarian. (That means that even if all librarians are introverted, all it takes is 1% of introverts among the salesmen to make the chances higher that Harry is a salesman.)

Do this:

Overlooking a simple data element can make our intuitions go completely astray. We keep mental images—simplifications of reality—that make us jump to conclusions before questioning assumptions or checking whether we have enough information.

Make your assumptions explicit. Don't take a problem statement as it is. Keep in mind that for every problem you're using implicit information—your assumptions. It's usually not hard to check the validity of assumptions, but first you need to know what they are.

Always favor hard data over mental simplifications.
Our preconceptions—such as stereotypes—can be useful in many situations, but we should always be careful not to over rely on them. When given the choice, always choose hard data.

6. Conformity: Everybody Else Is Doing It

In a series of experiments, researchers asked students in a classroom some very simple questions and, sure enough, most of them got the answers right. In another group, they asked the same questions but this time, there were actors posing as students, purposefully pushing wrong answers. In this instance, many more students provided wrong answers based on the leads from the actors.

This "herd instinct" exists—to different degrees—in all of us. Even if we hate to admit it, other people's actions do heavily influence ours. We fear looking dumb; failing along with many people is frequently not considered a big deal, but when we fail alone, we must take all the heat ourselves. There's always peer pressure to adopt the behaviors of the groups we're in.

This tendency to conform is notoriously exploited in advertising. Businesses often sell us products not based on their features, but by showing how popular they are. Since others are buying it in droves, why would we not join them?

Conformity is also one of the main reasons why, once a book makes it on a best-sellers' list, it tends to "lock in" and continues there for a long time. People like to consume what "everybody else" is consuming.

Do this:

Discount the influence of others. When analyzing information, shield yourself from others' opinions—at least at first. This is the best way to decide without being subconsciously swayed by popular opinions.

Beware of "social proof." Always raise a flag when someone tries to convince you by arguing primarily on the popularity of a choice, instead of on its merit.

Be courageous. Be willing to overcome obstacles and defend your viewpoints, despite their unpopularity.

7. Illusion of control: Shooting in the dark

Have you noticed that the vast majority of lotto players pick their own numbers instead of using the sometimes-available 'auto-pick' option (where the point of sales terminal chooses the numbers for you)? We all know that however the numbers are chosen doesn't change the chance of winning, so why the strong preference for picking our own numbers?

Curiously, even in situations we clearly can't control, we still tend to irrationally believe that we can somehow influence results. We just love to feel in control.

It's easier to illustrate this trap with games of chance, but the tendency to overestimate our personal control of events influences every aspect of our daily lives.

Unfortunately, contrary to the lotto example above, the outcomes of our decisions are usually complex and interconnected.

CHAPTER 3 WHY CAN'T I REMEMBER?

It's hard to assess to what extent we're responsible for the results we get. While some of the outcomes can be traced back to our own choices, a part of them will surely remain out of our direct control.

Do this:

> **Understand that randomness is part and parcel of life.** Although it may be hard to fathom or admit, some things are just random—in the sense that they don't depend on your effort at all. Accept responsibility for the things you can influence, but know that for many other things there is not much you can do. Better than assuming or expecting that every event is under your control, consciously choose how you respond.
>
> **Beware of superstitions.** Consider how many of your decisions are based on things you cannot really explain. Make those unknowns explicit and put them under scrutiny—instead of pretending you can control them.

8. Coincidence: We suck at probabilities

John Riley is a legend. He won a one-in-a-million-chance lottery...twice! That makes it a 1-in-a-trillion event. Does that mean the lottery was rigged or that John must have been singled out by Lady Luck?

Neither. If, throughout the years, 1000 lottery winners keep playing at least 100 times, attempting the "miracle" of winning it once more, that creates a 10% chance someone will win it again.

This means the "miracle" is not only possible but given enough attempts—its likelihood increases to a point of becoming almost inevitable.

Another classic example: it takes a group of just 23 people to make it more likely than not that two of them share the same birthday (day and month). That's how unintuitive probabilities are.

Do this:

> **Don't over-rely on gut estimates.** While useful, gut estimates will sometimes be way off the mark. Make sure you properly discount their importance, or that you understand the ramifications of trusting them.
>
> **Beware of "after the fact" probabilities.** One thing is the probability of someone having won the lottery twice—looking at it in retrospect. Another completely different view is that a particular person—chosen before the outcome—wins it. That would indeed qualify as a one-in-a-trillion event—and would make anyone seriously doubt the legitimacy of that lottery.

9. Recall: Not all memories are created equal

What's your best guess of the probability of a randomly selected airplane flight ending in a fatal crash? While many people grossly overestimate it, MIT studies show that, in reality, these fatal accidents happen at a rate of only 1 in 10,000,000. The fact that people suck at estimating probabilities explains only partially the tendency to overestimate. If you ask the same question right after a major airplane accident, be prepared for even more biased assessments.

CHAPTER 3 WHY CAN'T I REMEMBER?

We analyze information based on experience, and on what we can remember from it. Because of that, we're overly influenced by occurrences that stand out from others, such as events with highly dramatic impact which happened recently. The more "special" an event is, the greater the potential to distort our thinking. Of course, no one ever bothers about the other 9,999,999 planes that arrived safely at their destinations—so there's nothing more natural than forgetting about them.

Do this:

Get hard data. Don't rely upon your memory if you don't have to. Use it, of course, but always endeavor to find data that confirms or discounts your recollection.

Be aware of your emotions. When analyzing information, try to isolate yourself emotionally from it, at least temporarily. If you're analyzing an event, pretend it happened a long time ago, or that it happened to someone unrelated to you. Likewise, if asking for opinions, find people who are not emotionally involved with them or the consequences

Beware the media. The media is notorious for exaggerating the importance of certain events while conveniently neglecting others. Always evaluate information on its relevance and accuracy, and not on how much exposure it gets.

10. Superiority: The average is above average
A study surveyed drivers, asking them to compare their driving skills to other people in the experiment. Almost all the participants (93%) rated themselves as 'above average'. With

few exceptions, people have much inflated views of themselves. We overestimate our skills and capabilities, leading to errors in judgment. After making ourselves aware of the many thinking traps, we may become susceptible to falling into a new trap: the belief that we're now immune to traps. Don't.

The best way to avoid thinking traps is awareness and constant vigilance. But beware; it's much, much easier to notice others falling into these traps than us.

Do this:

Be humble. Always remember that everyone has blind spots.

Surround yourself with honest people. If we all have blind spots, there's nothing better than having honest people around us to point them out to us.

Don't go overboard. "Thinking traps" are inherent parts of us: they make us human. Applying rigorous and rational thinking to our decisions is important, but that doesn't mean that intuition has completely lost its place. Knowing about our own thinking traps is very useful—just don't get too worked up about it.

The studies that back up the data for this chapter can be found in a Wikipedia article, List of Cognitive Biases, as well in a book about decision making, Smart Choices, by John S. Hammond, Ralph Keeney, and Howard Raiffa. Another book used as a knowledge reference is Thomas Gilovich's How We Know What Isn't so.

CHAPTER 4
THE SEVEN SINS OF MEMORY

SIN OF OMISSION	1	Transience
	2	Absent-mindedness
	3	Blocking
SINS OF COMMISSION	4	Misattribution
	5	Suggestibility
	6	Bias
UNWANTED RECOLLECTIONS	7	Persistence

You didn't know memory was a sin?

The first three of the seven sins of memory can be thought of as **SINS OF OMISSION**, that is, different types of forgetting.

> The first sin, **Transience,** refers to the tendencies for memories to weaken over time, decreasing their accessibility.

> The second sin, **Absent-mindedness**, refers to lapses of attention that result in forgetting to do things. We all experience this kind of irritating, everyday forgetfulness when we cannot recall where we placed our eyeglasses or when we temporarily lose our car in a crowded parking lot.

> The third sin, **Blocking,** refers to cases in which information has not faded out of memory but is temporarily inaccessible for a variety of reasons. The most common example of blocking is probably the "tip of the tongue" experience, where we temporarily cannot retrieve a name or word that we are certain we know.

In contrast, the next three sins can be thought of as **SINS OF COMMISSION,** those instances in which memory is present but wrong.

> The fourth sin, **Misattribution,** occurs when we remember that something happened to us, but attribute the memory to an incorrect source. We might recall, for example, that we heard a fact on the radio, when it was instead told to us by a friend. Or, we might have only imagined doing something but then mistakenly come to believe that we've actually done it, sometimes resulting in a phenomenon called false recognition.
>
> The fifth sin, the second in this group, **Suggestibility,** refers to implanted memories, often generated by leading questions or suggestions that lead us to believe things about ourselves, sometimes entire events that never actually occurred.
>
> The sixth sin, the third of the Sins of Commission, is **Bias.** It refers to the ways our current knowledge and beliefs can distort our memories for the past. What we know and believe about ourselves in the present can be a powerful lens through which we view the past.

Finally, the last group represents **UNWANTED RECOLLECTIONS.**

> The seventh sin, **Persistence,** refers to unwanted recollections that people cannot forget. Persistent sins tend to be traumatic experiences that haunt our memories. They cannot be expunged from our mind.

CHAPTER 4 THE SEVEN SINS OF MEMORY

In extreme cases, they become self-defining recollections that permanently color our view of the present, past, and future. They are like the intrusive memories sometimes experienced by war veterans or survivors of sexual assault.

This chapter is based on the work of authors Daniel L. Schacter, Joan Y. Chiao, and Jason P. Mitchell, Department of Psychology, Harvard University, Cambridge, Massachusetts 02138.

CHAPTER 5
MEMORY MYTHS

You might think you are one of those people who is stuck forever with a bad memory. Not true.

Even people with "bad" memories can do something about it. It is a myth that your memory cannot be improved. Your memory definitely can be improved, no matter who you are. Awareness and understanding are the keys to memory skill.

Here are the 10 most common memory myths:

Myth 1 - Memory is a thing

Your memory is not a thing. There is no part of your brain that a doctor can point to and say, "There's a healthy-looking memory." Instead, memory is a process. You should think of remembering as an activity rather than in terms of a good memory or a bad memory.

So, like with any activity, you may remember well or remember poorly. But it is important to realize, just like with any skill, you can learn ways to do it better.

There is a second half to this memory myth. There is no single place in your brain where each memory is stored. Individual memories are actually the total of many different memories such as the sound of the thing, or the way it looks.

Each part of a memory is stored in different ways and in different places in your brain. Even the same types of memories are remembered differently. For example, a person might be able to remember a conversation but not be able to recall a simple music melody. So is memory a "thing" in your head? Definitely not!

Myth 2 - There is a secret to a good memory

Many people want to know the one secret to improving their memory. The truth is there is no one best way to improve your memory.

Think of it like this: Suppose I showed you a hammer and told you the hammer is a wonderful tool for pounding nails. Then you ask, "But how can I use that hammer to cut boards?" Obviously, you would not use a hammer to cut boards; you would use a saw. And to build a house, you would need several different types of tools. The same is true with memory.

There are memory techniques you can use to memorize different types of information. But there is no single "secret" method. In fact, the memory skills are not even secrets. Most of the memory methods have been around for more than 3,000 years. No one has the right to say they "invented" a particular memory skill or that the method is a secret.

The thing to realize is there is no quick fix for improving your memory. But you can improve your memory a lot by learning and applying the different methods you need.

Myth 3 - There is an easy way to memorize

People looking for the secret to a good memory often also think there is an easy way to memorize. If they could just learn the "trick," then remembering would not require any effort.

Memorizing is a learned skill. There is no easy, effortless way to do it. So you need to decide whether you are willing to give the mental effort required.

What memory methods do is make memorizing a lot more effective. The methods still require mental effort on your part. Think of it like this: If you wanted to learn how to play golf, or drive a car, or any other skill, would you expect there to be just one, easy way to do that activity?

Memory is the same. Since remembering is a skill, it requires effort. And you must learn and use the right techniques. If you learn the memory methods, you will remember much better. A person with an average IQ who learns memory methods will do better on objective tests than a high-IQ person who does not use memory methods.

Myth 4 - Some people are stuck with bad memories

First, you don't even have a memory (see Myth 1). But even if you look at memory as a skill or ability, it is not true you are stuck with the memory you have.

There are differences between people in natural memory ability. But these differences are much less important than the memory skills a person has learned.

For example, think of memory as a cardboard box. A person with a good natural memory may have a large box, while a person with a weaker memory might have a small box. As each person learns something new, they write the information on an index card. The person with the big box might just throw each card into the box, while the person with the small box might file each card neatly in alphabetical order.

Who do you think will remember things better? Even though the person with the poor natural memory has a smaller "box," since they've organized the information, they can find it (remember it) easily.

So, using memory skills, the memories in your mind are filed in an organized way and can be retrieved. Of all the memory myths, believing you are stuck with a bad memory is one of the worst because it stops you from trying. Don't believe it—you can improve your memory.

Myth 5 - Some people have photographic memories

It is very unlikely that there are more than just a few people in the world with photographic memories. This is just another of the memory myths. When most people who perform memory feats are tested, it turns out they are usually using memory techniques to remember information.

For example, in a demonstration using memory techniques, the memory "expert" tells the audience he will memorize the first 50 pages of any magazine in a specific period. When tested, he can remember what article is on every page, the pictures on the pages, the authors of the articles, the name of the main character on page 17, and so on. He can answer almost any question about the magazine. Audience members often ask him if he has a photographic memory?

He does not. He uses memory skills to study and memorize the magazine. This is something anyone can do. So don't worry about whether someone else has a photographic memory. Using memory skills, you can develop your own memory so that people will think you have one!

Myth 6 - You are too old or too young to improve your memory

You may have heard someone say they were too old to learn. This is another false memory myth. While it is true some people find remembering more difficult as they age, anyone can learn new things. **An elderly person who uses memory skills can actually remember better than a 20-year-old who does not!**

Children as young as 7 years old have been taught memory techniques. No matter your age, you still have the ability to learn.

Myth 7 - Memory is like a muscle and benefits from exercise

There is no evidence that simply memorizing over and over will improve your memory. What will improve your memory is practice using memory techniques. One classic study discovered that three hours of memorizing did not improve long-term memory, but three hours of practice using memory techniques did improve long-term memory.

Many memory books claim memory is a muscle and should be exercised. Scientists continue to research this premise. So rather than blindly practicing rote memorization, learn the memory techniques!

Myth 8 - A trained memory never forgets

Some people think that once they train their memory, they will never forget anything they see, do, or hear. The truth is that

CHAPTER 5 MEMORY MYTHS

once you train your memory, you will be able to remember things you want to remember. However, even with memory skills, you will still forget things. But you will remember things better than other people, and you will remember things better than you used to.

Research suggests that no one ever forgets anything. Everything we experience is buried deep in our minds. The problem is that we cannot get the information out when we need it. Memory skills give you the "hook" that lets you get the information out when you need it.

Myth 9 - Remembering too much can clutter your mind

Your ability to remember things does not depend on how much information is in your mind. Actually, it depends on how well organized the information is. Our brains can store an almost unlimited amount of information. But if the information in your mind is disorganized, it will be harder to remember things.

In some ways, the more you learn about something, the easier it is to learn more about it. Someone who is an expert on a subject has an easier time learning new facts about it than someone unfamiliar with the subject.

Learning new things does not "fill up" the mind. The storage capacity of your memory is virtually unlimited.

So don't be shy or afraid of learning.

Myth 10 - People only use 10 percent of their mind

You may have heard that most people only use about 10% (or less) of their brain. It turns out there is no research to support this. Scientists do not agree on how to measure brainpower and memory. So no one can accurately say how much of our brains we do not use. The important point is that most people probably don't use all of their brain's potential. By training our memories, we can improve our learning and memory skills. Whether we use 1%, 10%, or 90% doesn't matter. By learning memory skills, we can improve our memory and brainpower if we make the effort.

CONVINCED?

PART 2
YOU CAN DO IT!

This is a fun part of the book. This section is intended to boost your self-confidence.

It will.

CHAPTER 6
THE BEST IS YET TO COME

Starting right now, older people can put their highly capable brains to maximum use.

It is possible to become more creative as you age. The opportunity to begin this exciting phase of life starts, generally, during the "Young Old" period and transitions into the "Old," and "Old-Old" eras. There are several identifiable periods you'll recognize.

Reassessment

The process begins at mid-life, usually with re-evaluation and reassessment. This is also the period when people become very aware of their mortality. A response is often feelings of angst that can turn into depression. Individuals begin to question where they are in their lives. Some describe this period as a "midlife crisis;" others see it as a beginning of a quest.

Liberation and New Explorations

Retirement (regardless of age, but corresponding to the "Young Old" classifications) represents liberation and the chance to experiment. It starts with freeing up of one's self and acquiescing to the urge to try new things. The question, "If not now, when?" can be responded to since work-a-day concerns no longer exist. This phase of life can be a very positive experience. A common response is to become an active volunteer, giving back to our communities.

Summing Up

This is a resolution phase (from the 70s through to the mid-80s). It is the "Young Old" to "Old" period of life when we want (and need) to determine life's meaning. We have a need to focus on autobiographical efforts. During this period, it is also common to intensify our efforts to give back what life has given us.

Celebration

This last phase is devoted to reflection and celebration (mid 80s until death, the "Old-Old" part of life). It is the time for encores, a time to evaluate newly developed perspectives and to find new avenues for self-expression.

Memory and Wisdom

Oldsters have much to teach others. Seniors have the wisdom younger adults lack. What is wisdom? For seniors, it involves basing one's forecast of the future on what has already taken place. It represents accumulated knowledge and experience. Wisdom and knowledge are the special gifts that older people have to share.

In this later stage of life people often become contemplative and better able to base decisions on a full range of available information, intuition and feelings. Memory becomes the true "foundation of wisdom" and represents changes taking place in the brain itself which, incidentally, begins to work more efficiently. Despite common perceptions, cognitive and intellectual abilities do not peak when we are young, but in midlife and beyond.

Social Intelligence

The ability to sustain old relationships and to build new ones is called "social intelligence." It almost always improves with age. The elderly want to stay as socially involved as any other group. Thanks to their natural emotional and social resiliency, the elderly often are better able to deal with others in a social context than the young.

There are indications that men, as they age, strive to increase their connections socially. Women, who are naturally more social, try to become involved in issues of social justice. Think of retirement planning as similar to the planning a young person does on entering college and chooses courses for the first time. Like college, retirement offers a plethora of choices.

Engage in activities with long durations

For example, join a book club that meets regularly. It is through such associations that new friends are made.

Retirement is also a period of giving something back.

Giving back is a crucial imperative for older people. To do so, staying active mentally and physically is just as important. Engaging in a continuous learning process is a priority.

Creative Activity

Many believe creativity peters out as people age. This is not true. Creativity, in its broadest sense, covers all realms of human activity. Plumbers, gardeners, bricklayers, and football coaches can be just as creative as artists and writers.

In summary, with age comes loss–loss of health, loss of position, loss of family, loss of friends and, ultimately, loss of life. Creative pursuits enable older people to deal with such losses. Being creative in old age is a wonderful prescription for staying healthy. Mind engaged, body engaged. An older person can have a remarkably rich and enjoyable life. Plan and organize your life to make it so.

To remain young even though physically old, three primary factors come into play:

Remain in control

Creative pursuits provide a feeling of mastery, a wonderful elixir.

Be socially engaged

People who stay engaged with others live longer and enjoy better health.

Be creatively involved

Creative activities are stimulating and entertaining, and make people feel good about themselves.

Articles and speeches by Gene Cohen, M.D., Ph.D. are the sources for this chapter. Dr. Cohen is an expert on aging; he heads George Washington University's Center on Aging, Health and Humanities. Previously, he was director of the National Institute on Aging

CHAPTER 7
ARE YOU JUST INTELLIGENT, OR ARE YOU A GENIUS?

As a senior, ask yourself, "How was I treated as I grew up?" This question relates primarily to the way your education was handled. Were you one of those who was treated as "intelligent" or a "genius?" (Don't worry if you don't know the answer to the question; most of us won't know this either. This distinction typically becomes more important in later years. However, if pressed for an answer, most of us would answer "No" to both questions.)

What are the signs in children that are precursors to creative achievement in adulthood? They stand out; in fact, most highly creative people are polymaths—they enjoy and excel at a range of challenging activities

> For instance, in a survey of scientists at all levels of achievement, only about one-sixth report engaging in a secondary activity of an artistic or creative nature, such as painting or writing non-scientific prose.

> In contrast, nearly all Nobel Prize winners in science have at least one other creative activity that they pursue seriously. Creative breadth is an important but understudied component of genius.

If you mention "intelligence," the average person assumes you are speaking of that top 1 or 2%, the group whose IQ score is over 145. However, most intelligence researchers don't focus on the top 1 or 2%. They look at the general population (whose average IQ score is 100), and generally focus their attention on the lower to middle portion of the distribution.

Why? One reason is because the correlations between individual abilities as measured on IQ tests and the actual overall ability level of the person taking the test are the strongest among those whose IQ scores are 110 and below.

Scientists looked at the attributes of successful, intelligent, creative people and figured out that they had something going for them that other highly intelligent people did not. They made this trait the difference between "intelligent" and "genius".

What is the definition of "intelligence?"

An IQ score?

Computational ability?

Being able to talk your way out of a speeding ticket?

Knowing how to handle a crisis effectively?

Arguing a convincing case before a jury?

Maybe all of the above.

Dr. Robert Sternberg believes that intelligence is comprised of three facets which he called the Triarchic Theory of Intelligence:

1. **Analytical Ability**, (determined by IQ tests).

2. **Creativity**, and

3. **Practical Ability,** (being able to use analytical skills and creativity to effectively solve novel problems).

Dr. Rex Jung, from the Mind Institute and the University of New Mexico in Albuquerque, published a paper in 2009 showing biochemical support for the *Triarchic Theory.* In a nutshell, **he found that intelligence (as most people measure it today)**

is not enough to set a person apart and raise them to the level of genius.

It is *creativity*, the essential component that not all intelligent people possess, that defines genius status.

Not all creative people are geniuses. In order to reach genius status, creativity is a necessary attribute. However, don't sell yourself short if you are just "intelligent;" you're still pretty special.

Someone could have an IQ of 170, yet get lost inside a paper bag, or not have the ability to hold a conversation with anyone other than a dog. What made a genius like Albert Einstein so far ahead of his intelligent scientist peers? The answer is creativity.

Creativity is the defining feature that separates mere intelligence from utter genius.

You will benefit from learning the various methods professionals use to memorize so your true intelligence can manifest itself. Start by learning the language your mind uses. If you do, you'll be able to tap into your full potential and develop a remarkable memory. It's easier than you think–and you'll actually have fun doing it. Use the methods described in this book.

Learning and applying memory techniques is a life-changing experience. It's not difficult to advance beyond amateur status, but a commitment is necessary.

Your Mind Thinks in Pictures

As the mind has evolved, the brain has become amazingly effective in dealing with data interpreted by the senses. It's a

CHAPTER 7 ARE YOU JUST INTELLIGENT, OR ARE YOU A GENIUS?

big area of study: *Sensory ecology* deals with how organisms obtain information about their environment. *Sensory neurons* are the nerve cells responsible for transmitting information about external stimuli. *Sensory perception* is the process of acquiring and interpreting sensory information. A *sensory receptor* is a structure that recognizes external stimuli, and the *Sensory System* is a part of the nervous system of organisms. It is by correctly interpreting the five human senses that the mind understands the environment and makes decisions.

Of the human senses (sight, hear, smell, taste, or touch), *sight has become the most developed and sophisticated.* For that reason, our brains have become extremely effective in storing and processing images. Our minds are really good at working with concrete, real-world objects. On the other hand, trying to memorize abstract symbols, such as words printed on a page, is very unnatural and inefficient. Words are useful units of communication that humans have created, but words are not how our brains are best used to process information.

Imagery is the real language of the mind. Images are your mind's vocabulary, the building blocks of its language.

If asked to think about a horse, what comes to mind? Is it the letters H-O-R-S-E in sequence? Of course not. It is the picture of a horse—you can even visualize its color. Don't dreams always come as images? Pictures are how your mind communicates. As we age, we begin worrying about the pictures in our mind. They seem to be disappearing, or fading, or changing. Older persons seem to be obsessed about forgetfulness. There are a lot of us worrying about our aging memories and more are joining the worriers every year. The Census Bureau estimates that:

By 2025, there'll be 7,300,000 persons 75 to 79 years old.

By 2030, there'll be about 8 million persons 70-74 years old,

By 2050, there'll be over 16 million adults 70-74 years old.

By 2050, 40% of 65-year-olds are likely to reach age 90!

That's a lot of us worrying!

Most seniors need to do nothing more than what you'll learn in this book to eliminate major concerns. You will be able to easily implement behavioral strategies and memory techniques that enhance everyday memory.

Before you know it, your mind will be sharp as a tack!

CHAPTER 8
YOU HAVE THE POWER!

Isn't it nice to know neuroscientists have discovered that adults' brains are constantly changing and our ability to increase our knowledge never stops? The buzzword for older adults is *"neuroplasticity."* It means we are capable of growing new neurons and connections as we age. And that means learning never stops.

But some of us have trouble remembering. In all likelihood, it's been a problem that started several years ago and just seems to be getting worse. The facts are we can change our habits and learn new ways to remember. Author Gene Cohen has come to these conclusions about older adults:

> Older people are able to make better use of both halves of the brain.

> The brains of the elderly feature more densely rich neural networks than those of people half their age. This is really good.

> Our emotions and memory enable us to have a sense of increased serenity as we age.

> With age comes wisdom and experience. (We knew that!) The elderly can learn just as readily as the young, and they can be just as creative.

> "Developmental intelligence" results from accumulated knowledge and experience. We've got that going for us!

This "You're just as good as you once were; maybe better!" may be new information for many. We have been incorrectly conditioned by books and movies to believe our capabilities decline as we age. Unless illness prevents it, we CAN remain in the game until we die!

To repeat information first mentioned in Chapter 2: for most of us, our lives have been divided into phases:

The first phase was your childhood, early youth and education.

The second phase represents the time you graduated from school or college, got a job, married, had children, and educated them.

As life expectancies continued to expand, the third phase of life (previously referred to as "Old") is now divided into sub periods.

The first sub-period of the third phase of life begins with retirement. It's called, "**Young Old**," and generally represents those aged 65 to 74. You may have skidded into retirement, getting ready for it a little at a time. Or you may have been forced into retirement by an unforgiving company. Or you have been without work for a long, long time, and finally took the income from Social Security and called yourself "retired."

The next sub-period, from 75 to 84, is called **"Old."** This is a major life segment, but not your last. This part of our lives worries us the most, so we want to be sure we can take advantage of these years.

The last sub-period is **"Old-Old."** These are the years after age 85. The number of "old-old" persons continues to grow and as life expectancies expand, it well may be necessary to add a fourth category, "Old-Old-Old."

CHAPTER 8 YOU HAVE THE POWER!

Beginning in the "Young Old" period, we polish the development of "social intelligence." We no longer have work to define us, so we look to other methods. We develop a set of "social intelligence" skills, such as the ability to sustain old relationships and build new ones. And we look to creative pursuits to keep us feeling young and fulfilled.

Older Brains

Scientists have learned something many of us will find truly surprising: *The brains of the elderly often can function more efficiently and with better results than the brains of younger people.* They say it's because continual mental activity throughout life stimulates the growth of neurons, and enhanced creativity is often a notable characteristic of the aging process.

It's true. The thinking and intellectual skills of the elderly can stay remarkably sharp into the most advanced old age. Numerous scientific studies indicate that the brains of the elderly, if not affected by illness or accident, work better in many ways than those of people in their 20s and 30s. The aging process does negatively affect the brain, but brains also gain numerous advantages as they age.

Our older brains are the repository of accumulated knowledge, experience, greater wisdom, and more profound insights.

Older brains are far more complex than younger brains. Decades of learning develop enhanced neuron connections which improve brain function. Also, continual mental activity throughout life stimulates the growth of more neurons. Interestingly, so does exercise.

This enhanced neural architecture translates into an increased ability to deal with emotional difficulties. Additionally, the limbic system (the brain structure of emotions and memory) becomes more serene with age. Thus, older people are generally less negative and are calmer in adversity.

The young can use only a small portion of their brains for specific cognitive functions. Older folks have been using their cognitive functions longer, so they have an advantage. Brainpower is boosted by constantly challenging the brain. A lot of things present challenges, such as learning a new language or musical instrument, engaging in physical exercise, remaining socially active, or embarking on a course of self-improvement. Seniors can do any of these things and more. **Individual development is as possible for people in their 90s as it is for 70-year olds!**

The challenge for seniors is to enhance "developmental intelligence." Developmental intelligence is marked by a maturation of capabilities like social skills, emotional intelligence, life experiences, and overall cognition. **Group these qualities together and call it wisdom.**

Our age has also equipped us with meaningful judgmental capabilities. For the same reason, we have perspective younger adults lack.

Developmental intelligence manifests itself in highly sophisticated forms of understanding which involve three distinct thinking styles which are almost exclusively the purview of seniors:

CHAPTER 8 YOU HAVE THE POWER!

Recognizing the importance of context ("Relativistic thinking").

Resolving the contradictions in opposed points of view ("Dialectical thinking").

Adopting a broad-gauge view of a situation ("Systematic thinking").

Aren't we lucky!

CHAPTER 9
WHY YOU DON'T REMEMBER

Einstein is remembered as having said that if he had one hour to save the world, he would spend fifty-five minutes defining the problem and only five minutes finding the solution.

The statement (whether the story is true or not) illustrates an important point: before jumping right into solving any problem (in our case, learning how to better remember), step back and stop! Invest the time and effort to improve your understanding of the problem. Try to see problems from many different perspectives. **This means that to remember easier, your first memory goal is to master the important steps in achieving memory excellence.** It starts with understanding the problem you're trying to overcome.

The Problem Is To Know What the Problem Is

Defining the problem is the focal point of memory improving efforts. As such, it makes sense to devote as much attention and dedication as possible to problem definition. What usually happens is that as soon as we have a problem to work on we're so eager to get to solutions that we neglect spending any time refining it.

What most of us don't realize—and what supposedly Einstein was alluding to—is that the quality of the solutions we come up with will be in direct proportion to the quality of the description of the problem we're trying to solve.

Your ability to connect ideas is critically important. Solutions to a well-defined problem will be more abundant and of higher quality if you can bring all your knowledge to the task. Being able to connect (link) ideas will make finding solutions much, much easier. Most importantly, the confidence you'll have by tackling a well-understood problem will substantially aid the development of solutions.

Problem Definition Tools and Strategies

The good news is that getting different perspectives and angles on a problem are skills that can be learned. As a result, remembering will be easier. Following are some strategies you can use to understand and correct whatever it is that's holding you back:

Rephrase the Problem

When a manufacturing executive asked employees to brainstorm ways to increase their productivity, all he got back were blank stares. They thought he was asking them to suggest ways to improve "his" job. When he rephrased his request a second time, asking for ways to make their jobs easier, he could barely keep up with the deluge of suggestions.

Words carry strong implicit meaning and as such, play a role in how we perceive a problem. In the example above, 'be productive' might create a mental picture of a sacrifice you're making for the company, while 'make your job easier' brings up all the ideas you've had for improving things for your own benefit, but from which the company also benefits. In the end, the problem is still the same, but the feelings—and the points of view—associated with each statement are quite different. The lesson is that when trying to remember anything, emphasize the personal value you'll gain; it will increase your motivation.

Play freely with your problem statement (the wild and crazy image you create also benefits from a little extra thought), rewording or re-imagining it several times. For a methodic and scholarly approach to a business event, take single words and substitute variations. For example, try replacing "increase sales" with 'attract', 'develop', 'extend', or 'repeat,' and see how your perception of the problem changes. A rich vocabulary is helpful, so use a thesaurus to expand your vocabulary. Do the same with the images you create. Choose the one that's the craziest and makes recall easier.

Expose and Challenge Assumptions

Every problem—no matter how apparently simple it may be—comes with a long list of assumptions. Many of these assumptions may be inaccurate and could make the memory response inadequate or even misguided.

Start by getting rid of very general assumptions. Make the statements explicit and easily understood. Write a list of as many assumptions as you can, especially those that may seem the most obvious and 'untouchable'. Do anything that brings more clarity to the event. Go further and test each assumption for validity: think in ways that might not be valid and examine the consequences. What you find may surprise you. You may discover your limitations are self-imposed.

See the Broader Picture

Each problem may be a small piece of a larger problem.

If overwhelmed with details or with the creation of an image that conveys your thought, look at it from a more general perspective. Ask questions such as, "*What is this part of?*" or "*What is this an example of?*" or "*What is the intention behind this?*" Then make your mental image.

One way to get a more general and broader view of your task is to replace words with hyponyms. Hyponyms are words that are a subcategory of a more general class. An easy test is to replace X and Y in a test sentence and see if the result makes sense. For example, "(X) a horse is a kind of (Y) animal" makes sense; but "An animal is a kind of horse" does not.

Hyponyms are words that describe things more specifically.

Niagara Falls is a hyponym for waterfall. Ford is a hyponym for car. Dog is a hyponym for animal. Daisy and rose are hyponyms of flower. Scarlet, vermilion, and crimson are hyponyms of red. Chair and table are hyponyms of furniture. Start with the big picture (top of the triangle) and break it down into the details.

See the Bigger Picture

If your problem is part of a greater problem, it also means that each problem is composed of many smaller problems. Breaking a problem into many smaller parts, each of them more specific than the original, can often provide great insights.

Here's how: Begin by identifying the words that refer to broad categories or general concepts, called *hypernyms*. **A hypernym is a word whose meaning includes the meanings of other words.** Hypernyms are words that are more generic and inclusive than a given word. Car is a hypernym for Toyota Camry.

Airplane is a hypernym for Boeing 747. Flower is a hypernym of daisy and rose. Primate is a hypernym for chimpanzee and human.

Once you see the bigger picture, you may not be so troubled.

Find Multiple Perspectives

Before rushing to solve a major memory problem, look at the issue from different perspectives. It's a great way to have instant insight into new, overlooked directions. For example, viewing the problem from your neighbor's point of view may result in recognizing a different "reality" that completely changes your understanding. It may make the memory picture easier to recall.

Redo the problem/memory statement many times, each time using one of the different perspectives. How would your garden club see this problem? Your children? Your mom? Also, imagine how people in various roles would frame the problem. How would a politician see it? A college professor? A nun? Try to find the differences and similarities of how the different roles would see your problem.

Use Effective Language

There isn't a one-size-fits-all formula for properly crafting the perfect problem/memory statement, but here are some language constructs that may help:

Assume a myriad of solutions. An excellent way to start a problem statement is with the assumption there are several solutions (images) possible: The expression, *"In what ways might"* is much superior to *"How can I?"* as it hints that there's a multitude of solutions, not just one, or maybe none. As simple as this sounds, the feeling of expectancy helps your brain find solutions.

Make it positive. Negative pictures or sentences require a lot more conscious intellectual activity to process and may slow down the development of a solution or derail the train of thought. Positive statements help find the real goal behind the problem and, as such, are much more motivating. For example: instead of creating an image depicting "quitting smoking," a better approach might be to develop an image that shows "increased energy and a longer, happier life."

Frame the memory problem in the form of a question. Our brain loves questions. If the question is powerful and engaging, our brains will do everything within their reach to answer it. We just can't help it: our brains will start working on the problem immediately and keep working in the background, even when we're not aware of it.

If still stuck, consider using the following formula for phrasing the problem statement: "In what ways might (action) (object) (qualifier) (end result)?" Example: picture the ways packaging (action) the book (object) more attractively (qualifier) might cause people to buy it (end result)?"

Make the Problem Statement Engaging

In addition to using effective language, it's important to come up with a problem/picture statement that is truly exciting. Doing so readies your mind for creatively tackling the problem. If the picture looks too dull, invest the time to add vigor to it while still keeping it genuine. Make it enticing. Your brain will thank (and reward) you later.

It's one thing to picture increasing sales **(boring);** a better picture is **wowing** your customers!

Reverse the Problem

When stuck with a problem, turn it on its head. If increasing the size of your church congregation is the objective, find out what would make you lose members. If struggling to find ways to picture increased sales, find ways to imagine decreasing them instead.

"Make more sales calls" may seem an evident way of increasing sales, but sometimes we only see obvious answers until we look at the problem from an opposite direction. This seemingly convoluted method may not seem intuitive at first, but turning a problem on its head can uncover rather obvious solutions to the original problem.

Gather Facts

If the history of your memory problem is your challenge, investigate causes and circumstances. Probe details about it; investigate its origins and causes. If the problem picture is vague, investigating facts is usually more productive, especially if the facts can be visualized.

Ask questions and gather facts. What is not known about it? Can the problem be diagramed? What are the problem boundaries? Be curious. Having a crazy, memorable image is even better.

Problem-Solve Your Problem Statement

Getting the right perspective of a problem is a problem in itself. Use any creative thinking technique. There are plenty to choose from.

Of course, it's hard to balance the time invested in defining the problem with the effort required to actually develop the problem solution. You can...with practice. In fact, when you start paying more attention to problem definition and the creation of a mental picture, you'll find it is usually much harder than solving the problem. But the payoff is well worth the effort.

A quick review:

Rephrase the problem

Expose and challenge assumptions

See the broader picture (your problem may be part of a larger problem, a hyponym)

See the big picture (your problem may include a broad category of issues, a hypernym)

See different perspectives

Phrase the problem statement in a questioning way

State the issues in an exciting way

Reverse the issue for perspective

Evaluate just the facts

And last of all…

Use your head!

CHAPTER 10
FUN WITH MEMORY

Maybe your mind isn't as sharp as it once was! Who says? It's just gotten older, that's all. Let's find out. These are objective quizzes.

Here are **20 "Sharp" Questions**. Aerage score is 12.

1. What builds strong bodies 12 ways?
   A. Flintstones vitamins
   B. The Buttmaster
   C. Spaghetti
   D. Wonder Bread
   E. Orange Juice
   F. Milk
   G. Cod Liver Oil

2. Before he was Mohamed Ali, he was...
   A. Sugar Ray Robinson
   B. Roy Orbison
   C. Gene Autry
   D. Rudolph Valentino
   E. Fabian
   F. Mickey Mantle
   G. Cassius Clay

3. Pogo, the comic strip character said, 'We have met the enemy and...
   A. It's you
   B. He is us
   C. It's the Grinch
   D. He wasn't home

CHAPTER 10 FUN WITH MEMORY

    E. He's really me and you

    F. We quit

    G. He surrendered

4. What's the famous sign off? Good night, David..

    A. Good night, Chet.

    B. Sleep well

    C. Good night, Irene

    D. Good night, Gracie

    E. See you later, alligator

    F. Until tomorrow

    G. Good night, Steve

5. You'll wonder where the yellow went...

    A. When you use Tide

    B. When you lose your crayons

    C. When you clean your tub

    D. If you paint the room blue

    E. If you buy a soft water tank

    F. When you use Lady Clairol

    G. When you brush your teeth with Pepsodent

6. Before he was the Skipper's Little Buddy, Bob Denver was Dobie's friend...

    A. Stuart Whitman

    B. Randolph Scott

    C. Steve Reeves

    D. Maynard G. Krebs

    E. Corky B. Dork

    F Dave the Whale

    G. Zippy Zoo

7. Liar, liar...

    A. You're a liar

    B. Your nose is growing

    C. Pants on fire

    D. Join the choir

    E. Jump up higher

    F. On the wire

    G. I'm telling Mom

8. Meanwhile, back in Metropolis, Superman fights a never-ending battle for truth, justice and...

    A. Wheaties

    B. Lois Lane

    C. TV rating

    D. World peace

    E. Red tights

    F. The American way

    G. News headlines

9. Hey kids! What time is it?

    A. It's time for Yogi Bear

    B. It's time to do your homework

    C. It's Howdy Doody Time

    D. It's bedtime

    E. The Mighty Mouse Hour

    F. Scooby Doo Time

10. Lions and tigers and bears....

    A. Yikes

    B. Oh, no

    C. Gee whiz

CHAPTER 10 FUN WITH MEMORY

   D. I'm scared
   E. Oh my
   F. Help! Help!
   G. Let's run

11. Bob Dylan advised us never to trust anyone...
   A. Over 40
   B. Wearing a uniform
   C. Carrying a briefcase
   D. Over 30
   E. You don't know
   F. Who says, 'Trust me'
   G. Who eats tofu

12. NFL quarterback who appeared in a television commercial wearing women's stockings...
   A. Troy Aikman
   B. Kenny Stabler
   C. Joe Namath
   D. Roger Staubach
   E. Joe Montana
   F. Steve Young
   G. John Elway

13. Brylcream...
   A. Smear it on
   B. You'll smell great
   C. Tame that cowlick
   D. Grease ball heaven
   E. It's a dream
   F. We're your team
   G. A little dab'll do ya

14. I found my thrill...
   A. In Blueberry muffins
   B. With my man, Bill
   C. Down at the mill
   D. Over the windowsill
   E. With thyme and dill
   F. Too late to enjoy
   G. On Blueberry Hill

15. Before Robin Williams, Peter Pan was played by...
   A. Clark Gable
   B. Mary Martin
   C. Doris Day
   D. Errol Flynn
   E. Sally Fields
   F. Jim Carrey
   G. Jay Leno

16. Name the Beatles...
   A. John, Steve, George, Ringo B. John, Paul, George, Roscoe
   C. John, Paul, Stacey, Ringo
   D. Jay, Paul, George, Ringo
   E. Lewis, Peter, George, Ringo
   F. Jason, Betty, Skipper, Hazel
   G. John, Paul, George, Ringo

17. I wonder, wonder
   A. Who ate the leftovers?
   B. Who did the laundry?
   C. Was it you?

CHAPTER 10 FUN WITH MEMORY

  D. Who wrote the book of love?

  E. Who I am?

  F. Who passed the test?

  G. Who knocked on the door?

18. I'm strong to the finish...

  A. Cause I eats my broccoli

  B. Cause I eats me spinach

  C. Cause I lift weights

  D. Cause I'm the hero

  E. And don't you forget it

  F. Cause Olive Oyl loves me

  G. To outlast Bluto

19. When it's least expected, you're elected; you're the star today.

  A. Smile, you're on Candid Camera

  B. Smile, you're on Star Search

  C. Smile, you won the lottery

  D. Smile, we're watching you

  E. Smile, the world sees you

  F. Smile, you're a hit

  G. Smile, you're on TV

20. What do M & M's do?

  A. Make your tummy happy!

  B. Melt in your mouth, not in your pocket

  C. Make you fat

  D. Melt your heart

  E. Make you popular

F. Melt in your mouth, not in your hand

G. Come in colors

The answers: to 20 Sharp Questions

1. D - Wonder Bread
2. G - Cassius Clay
3. B - He is us
4. A - Good night Chet
5. G - When you brush your teeth with Pepsodent
6. D - Maynard G. Krebs
7. C - Pants on fire
8. F - The American Way
9. F - It's Howdy Doody Time
10. E - Oh my
11. D - Over 30
12. C - Joe Namath
13. G - A little dab'll do ya
14. G - On Blueberry Hill
15. B - Mary Martin
16. G - John, Paul, George, Ringo
17. D - Who wrote the Book of Love
18. B - Cause I eats me spinach
19. A - Smile, you're on Candid Camera
20. F - Melt in your mouth, not in your hand

"Out Of The Box" Teasers

Here are 10 questions that might not test your intelligence as much as your ability to "think out of the box."

1. A man lives on the 28th floor of a high-rise building. Every day he gets the elevator down to the ground floor to

CHAPTER 10 FUN WITH MEMORY

leave the building to go to work. Upon returning from work, he always gets out at the 26th floor and climbs the other two floors unless it's raining! Why?

2. A man and his son are in a car accident. The father dies on the spot, but the boy is rushed to the hospital. When he arrives the surgeon says, "I can't operate on this boy, he is my son!" How can this be?

3. A woman had two sons who were born on the same hour of the same day of the same year. But they were not twins. How could this be so?

4. A murderer is condemned to death. He has to choose between three rooms. The first is full of raging fires, the second of assassins with loaded guns, and the third of lions that haven't eaten in three years. Which room is the safest for him to go to?

5. Can you name three consecutive days without using the words "Monday, Tuesday, Wednesday, Thursday, Friday, Saturday, or Sunday" (or day names in any other language)?

6. A London cab driver picked up a lady who was a notorious chatterbox. He did not want to engage in conversation, so he pretended to be deaf and dumb. He pointed to his mouth and ears to indicate that he could neither speak nor hear. After she alighted, he pointed to the meter so that she could see how much she owed. She paid him and walked off. Then she realized that he could not have been a deaf mute. How did she know?

7. There are six eggs in the basket. Six people each take one of the eggs. How can it be that one egg is left in the basket?

8. Anthony and Cleopatra are lying dead on the floor of a room. Nearby is a broken bowl. There is no mark on either of their bodies, and they were not poisoned. How did they die?

9. The boss of a storage warehouse had just arrived at work when one of his employees burst into his office. The man said that while asleep in the building the previous night he had dreamt that one of the stored boxes contained a bomb which would explode at two p.m. The boss was skeptical, but agreed to investigate. After a search, a bomb was truly found in the area foreseen in the man's dream. The police were called to defuse the bomb and thus a tragedy was averted. Yet afterwards, the boss, after thanking the employee profusely, fired him. The sacked man had not planted the bomb, and his prophetic dream had saved the warehouse from a tragedy. Yet the manager was right to fire him. How could that be so?

10. A poor servant in a village was told by his master that he could wish for anything he wanted. It could be any wish at all but just one. The servant asked his mother what she wanted, and she said she wanted a TV set. Next, the servant asked his wife who said she wanted a microwave. Finally, the servant went to his father who wanted a bicycle. The next day he went to his master and made one wish through which his mother, father, and wife each got what they wanted. What was his wish?

Answers to the 10 **"Out of the Box" questions**

1. The man is very short and can only press the button for the 26th floor. However, if it is raining then he will have his umbrella with him to press the higher button.

CHAPTER 10 FUN WITH MEMORY

2. The surgeon was his mother.

3. They were two of a set of triplets (the third being a girl). Of course, they can also be two of quadruplets, etc.).

4. The third. Lions that haven't eaten in three years would certainly have been dead.

5. Yesterday, Today, and Tomorrow!

6. He couldn't be deaf as he must have heard her instructions when she entered his taxi, or he wouldn't have known where to take her.

7. The last person took the basket with the eggs still inside.

8. Anthony and Cleopatra were actually the names of two goldfish. The bowl was knocked over by a cat, and they were left without water.

9. Because he was the night watchman (or some other night shift worker) and had been sleeping on his job.

10. Since it could be any wish at all, he asked for three wishes, thus satisfying everybody! Of course, he could also simply ask for a sum large enough to allow him to buy all the three items.

A Quiz For Know-it-alls

This is a quiz for people who know everything! These are not trick questions. They are straight questions with straight answers.

1. Name the one sport in which neither the spectators nor the participants know the score or the leader until the contest ends.

2. What famous North American landmark is constantly moving backward?

3. Of all vegetables, only two can live to produce on their own for several growing seasons. All other vegetables must be replanted every year. What are the only two perennial vegetables?

4. What fruit has its seeds on the outside?

5. In many liquor stores, you can buy pear brandy, with a real pear inside the bottle. The pear is whole and ripe, and the bottle is genuine; it hasn't been cut in any way. How did the pear get inside the bottle?

6. Only three words in standard English begin with the letters ' dw' and they are all common words. Name two of them.

7. There are 14 punctuation marks in English grammar. Can you name at least half of them?

8. Name the only vegetable or fruit that is never sold frozen, canned, processed, cooked, or in any other form except fresh.

9. Name 6 or more things that you can wear on your feet beginning with the letter 'S.'

Answers to the Quiz for Know-It-Alls

1. The one sport in which neither the spectators nor the participants know the score or the leader until the contest ends: Boxing.

CHAPTER 10 FUN WITH MEMORY

2. North American landmark constantly moving backward: Niagara Falls . The rim is worn down about two and a half feet each year because of the millions of gallons of water that rush over it every minute.

3. Only two vegetables that can live to produce on their own for several growing seasons: Asparagus and rhubarb.

4. The fruit with its seeds on the outside: Strawberry.

5. How did the pear get inside the brandy bottle? It grew inside the bottle. The bottles are placed over pear buds when they are small, and are wired in place on the tree. The bottle is left in place for the entire growing season. When the pears are ripe, they are snipped off at the stems.

6. Three English words beginning with dw: dwarf, dwell and dwindle...(Dwight is another.)

7 Fourteen punctuation marks in English grammar: Period, comma, colon, semicolon, dash, hyphen, apostrophe, question mark, exclamation point, quotation mark, brackets, parenthesis, braces, and ellipses (An ellipsis is a series of three points with spaces between them... inserted into a quotation to indicate the omission of material from the original quotation).

8. The only vegetable or fruit never sold frozen, canned, processed, cooked, or in any other form but fresh: Lettuce.

9. Six or more things you can wear on your feet beginning with 'S': Shoes, socks, sandals, sneakers, slippers, skis, skates, snowshoes, stockings, stilts.

The Checkup Quiz

First question: you are a participant in a race. You overtake the second person. What position are you in?

Second question: if you overtake the last person, then you are....?

Third question involves very tricky arithmetic! Note: this must be done in your head. Do not use paper and pencil or a calculator.

> Take 1000 and add 40 to it. Now add another 1000. Now add 30. Add another 1000. Now add 20 . Now add another 1000. Now add 10. What is the total?

Fourth question: Mary's father has five daughters: 1. Nana, 2. Nene, 3. Nini, 4.. Nono, and ???. What is the name of the fifth daughter?

Fifth question: A mute person goes into a shop and wants to buy a toothbrush. By imitating the action of brushing his teeth, he successfully expresses himself to the shopkeeper, and the purchase is done. Next, a blind man comes into the shop who wants to buy a pair of sunglasses. How does he indicate what he wants?

Answers to the Check Up Quiz

First answer: if you answered that you are first, then you are absolutely wrong! If you overtake the second person and you take his place, you are in second place!

Second answer: if you answered that you are second to last, then you are...wrong again. How can you overtake the last person??

CHAPTER 10 FUN WITH MEMORY

Third answer: Did you get 5000? The correct answer is actually 4100...

Fourth answer: Did you answer Nunu? No! Of course it isn't. Her name is Mary! Read the question again!

Fifth question answer: It's really very simple: he opens his mouth and asks for it...

Visual Perception

How many arrows do you see?

The Kanizsa Triangle Illusion

A triangle is perceived even though it is not actually there.

Face or Vase

The Ponzo Illusion

Two identically sized lines appear to be different sizes when placed over parallel lines that seem to converge as they recede into the distance.

Hermann Grid Illusion

The white dots at the center of each square seem to shift from white to gray.

CHAPTER 10 FUN WITH MEMORY

Zöllner illusion

Straight lines appear to move even though they are static.

The Ames Room Illusion

Two people standing in a room appear to be of dramatically different sizes, even though they are the same size.

CHAPTER 10 FUN WITH MEMORY

The Spinning Dancer Illusion

To see the dancing girl spin either left or right, go to the web site, http: //www.1 23opticalilusions.com/pages/Spinning Dancer.php

This optical illusion reveals how our brain processes visual information in order to create a visual model of the world. Our visual system evolved to make certain assumptions that are almost always right (like, if something is smaller is it likely farther away). But these assumptions can be exploited to create a false visual construction, or an optical illusion and trick our mind. The spinning girl image is not objectively "spinning" in one direction or the other. It is a two-dimensional image that is simply shifting back and forth. Our brains did not evolve to interpret two-dimensional representations of the world but the actual three-dimensional world. Our mind assumes we are looking at a 3-D image and uses clues to interpret it as such. Without adequate clues it may just arbitrarily decide a best fit—spinning clockwise or counterclockwise. And once this fit is chosen, the illusion is complete – we see a 3-D spinning image.

PART 3
DO IT!

This is where the rubber hits the road. You're primed and ready to learn tried and true memory methods. Thousands of people have proved to themselves that their memory is as good as the next guy's. Maybe better.

Believe me, developing a great memory is not an impossible task. You can have a memory that's sharp as a tack (well, maybe not that sharp)!

Why are there so many different ways to remember?

Think of the methods as tools. You use a different tool for different tasks. You wouldn't use a shovel to pound nails, or a pair of pliers to cut a board.

Get ready to fill your tool box with memory methods.

CHAPTER 11
MEMORY TECHNIQUES VOCABULARY

OK. We're ready now to start learning the methods of memory professionals. This chapter is an introduction to the systems and terms that will help you remember better. It starts out with brief explanations of the most popular memory words professionals use. The memory systems best for seniors are described in detail in subsequent chapters.

Improving recall has been of interest to civilizations since the days of the Romans. In more recent times, feats of memory have been exploited by professionals, leading us to believe a fantastic memory was either a magic trick or a gift of birth. It's only in the contemporary period that memory techniques have been accepted as tools anyone can learn to use to enhance memory performance.

One major development is the scientific acceptance that exercising our brain is just like exercising our muscles. (Remember "*neuroplasticity*" from Chapter 8? It means we are capable of growing new neurons and connections as we age. For you and me, it **means learning never stops.)**

When we do things with our minds, just what is intended occurs: we get better. Defining what constitutes "brain exercise" is still a scientific endeavor, but you'll get a brain workout for certain as you progress through the chapters of this book.

The words starting on page 88 are the vocabulary you'll use as you work to overcome or prevent the memory problems attributed to old age. Old age is not an acceptable excuse for forgetfulness. The mind is able to grow throughout life. Older

CHAPTER 11 MEMORY TECHNIQUES VOCABULARY

persons can systematically learn memory techniques and incorporate them into daily activities. Use these techniques to become an ace at remembering things. It's easy.

Beginning on the following page are the significant terms memory professionals use and describe in their publications.

The sources most referenced for these definitions are: The Brilliant Memory Book (Dominic O'Brien); Memory Book (by Harry Lorayne and Jerry Lucas); Achieving Optimal Memory (Arron Nelson and Gary Small), The Memory Bible (Aaron P. Nelson), Your Memory (Kenneth B. Higbee), Ageless Memory (Harry Lorayne), and Moonwalking with Einstein (Joshua Foer). Of course, there are many other authors.

Association	The way new information can best be remembered is by consciously associating it with something already known or remembered. Virtually all learning is based on memory. All memory is based on visualization and association You can remember any new piece of information if it is vividly associated to something you already know or remember. Learning how to associate new to known is the key to a trained memory.
Chunking	Chunking is an organizational method of breaking a large group of items into subgroups. "1234567890" chunked would be "123-456-7890."
Interaction	Interaction is the association of two items and the creation of a connection between them. One of the images must be doing something to or with the other image. Each part of the unit serves as a cue for remembering the rest of the unit.
Link	A Link is used to remember things in sequence. One item "links" to another. Linking utilizes Substitution, Out of Proportion, Exaggeration, and Action. Links that make use of the five senses are best. A link must lead from one item to the next.

CHAPTER 11 MEMORY TECHNIQUES VOCABULARY

Memory Palace (also known as "Journey Method" or "Method of Loci")	The concept is based on a skill each of us has: we're very good at remembering details of places we know. A "Memory Palace" is a metaphor for places you can easily visualize, like the rooms in your home and things that are in that room.

Making the journey from one familiar spot to another is a way to store and recall all kinds of information. Using a familiar route's memorable features as a peg and associating new information to the peg combines the techniques of association, location, and imagination.

Ancient Greeks devised the technique. The concept is extremely useful for managing complex or lengthy material like a speech without notes or a PowerPoint presentation. For a speech, each main talking point is related to the succession of rooms or landmarks on the journey. The details associated with a main point of the speech (the location) trigger recall of related information. |
| Mind Map | Mind Mapping organizes material on a particular subject as you think laterally, creatively, and randomly about it. By building a picture of ideas as they come to you, you establish logical connections and sequences for thoughts. |

Mnemonics	The word, *mnemonic* (the first m is silent), is derived from Mnemosyne, the Greek goddess of memory. A mnemonic is a device used to assist recall and information retention. The use of mnemonics is based on the observation that spatial, personal, surprising, physical, sexual, humorous, or otherwise 'relatable' information is more easily remembered by the human mind than abstract or impersonal forms of information. Mnemonic devices are effective for remembering list-like information used repeatedly over time. For example, when you were in school you learned the mnemonic, "All cows eat grass" for the notes (a,c,e,g) that fall on the spaces of the base-clef musical staff. Mnemonics work.
Objective memory	An indicator of memory performance in ways that can be measured.
Peg	A system for remembering phone numbers, addresses, numerical sequences, or lists by visualizing objects and pairing them with a peg (usually an object that can be recalled in a numbered sequence). Pegging is a way to establish location in a numbered list. Thoughts are tied to a tangible image of a number and thus able to be recalled at specific points. Pegging is a good system for seniors.
Phonetic Alphabet	Phonetic alphabets are sets of symbols that represent individual sounds in written form.
Scamper	"Scamper" is a mnemonic that stands for: Substitute, Combine, Adapt, Modify, Put to another use, Eliminate, Reverse—all part of the process of committing facts, ideas, or thoughts to memory.

CHAPTER 11 MEMORY TECHNIQUES VOCABULARY

SQ3R Method	SQ3R stands for Survey, Question, Read, Recite, and Review. The method is useful for integrating and remembering information from a textbook or lengthy professional material. It is easier said than done.
Subjective memory	Subjective memory represents the perception of memory performance. Subjective memory is not measurable.
Substitution	Substitution is the process where an intangible or abstract object is replaced by an image that is ridiculous, wild, out of proportion, extravagant, in a huge quantity, that sounds like or is reminiscent of the item, and that can be pictured in the mind and linked to something already in your memory. Substitution is essential to the memory process.
Visualization	Visualization is the joining of two images together in an outlandish manner. A retrievable memory placement occurs when a new visual image is associated with another image already stored in the brain. Visualized images must be associated/joined. Side-by-side doesn't work. Substitute and integrate the images into the most bizarre, graphic way you can think of. Substitution, visualization, and association work together to create recallable memories.

There are many sources of information about memory techniques. Google or Bing "memory techniques," or similar words, to explore them.

CHAPTER 12
SURVEY, QUESTION, READ, RECITE, AND REVIEW

Who doesn't want to keep their brain young? You **must** believe it. You can be mentally active for a long, long time. You have the ability to do that; in fact, you have more control than you think. There are things you can do to keep your brain young. You can continue to exercise your brain muscle until your death. It's never too late to protect your brain cells and delay memory decline. Start by gaining an understanding of the best ways to become a "memory whiz."

We evaluate memory two ways: either subjectively or objectively (first mentioned in Chapter 2):

> **Subjective memory** represents our perception of how well we do. Subjective memory is not measurable
>
> **Objective memory** is an indicator of how well we perform in ways that can be measured. Objective evaluation counts.

The SQ3R Method

Making objective memory function at its best utilizes the "SQ3R Method." Understanding is critical to the improvement process. SQ3R is the technique that will help you master any topic. It may appear the method is cumbersome, but if understanding and remembering are important to you, learning to use this method will be time well spent.

An "S," a "Q," and "3 R's" Translated

S—Survey

> Gain an overview of the material via a quick skim or read-through—**a survey.** Reading chapter headings and

subheadings or the first sentence of each paragraph will yield a general mental outline of the material. Look over graphics, including figures, images, and diagrams. If the material contains a concluding summary and associated study questions, read them.

Q — Question

The second step: **question** yourself about what you've just read. Formulate provocative and interesting questions based on the main points gleaned from your initial survey. Then, when you read the material fully in the next step, curiosity will galvanize your focus and your previously prepared questions will enable you to better absorb what you read.

R — Read

Carefully **read** the material for comprehension. Think about your questions. Note taking and underlining should be minimal; focus only on key concepts. Taking too many notes at this point can interrupt the flow of information and degrade your comprehension.

R — Recite

Speak aloud about what you've just read, either to yourself or to someone else. **Recite** it. This is an excellent means of checking comprehension and deepening understanding of the material.

R — Review

Come back to the material a day or so later. **Review** any notes made. Ask yourself how what you've read complements or contradicts other information on the subject. Finally, return to your questions. How would you answer them now? What questions are you left with? Review the material briskly several more times over the course of the next week or weeks. Spaced rehearsal will promote effective memory consolidation and retention.

Remembering what you've read gets easier after going through these steps. Use one of the memory techniques to cement your knowledge of the subject.

The definitions in this chapter were developed from statements by various writers.

CHAPTER 13
MNEMONICS

We remember two ways: The first is the "natural" memory we are born with. It is the one that everyone uses automatically and without thinking. The second is our "artificial" memory. Artificial memory has to be trained and developed through the learning and practicing of a variety of techniques. Natural memory is better...and easier. Using mnemonics help natural memory.

Mnemonics is the art of assisting natural memory by using a system of artificial aids to help in the recall of names, dates, facts, and figures. It is a learning technique that aids natural information retention by translating information into a form (pictures, letters, rhymes, and words) the human brain can better retain. The use of mnemonics is based on the observation that relatable information, rather than more abstract or impersonal forms of information, is much easier recalled. Mnemonics are more effective for anyone who struggles with remembering or has a weak long-term memory.

The word is hard to pronounce and is not used in everyday conversation, but you're who you are today because of mnemonics. You can't become a memory whiz without understanding mnemonics. The human mind more easily remembers mnemonic information that relates to the visual perception (pictures) of objects in front of us. Names, dates, facts, figures—anything will be more easily remembered if made into an image that is personal, surprising, physical, sexual, humorous, or otherwise relatable.

The mind makes these mental pictures by using mnemonic techniques; the result is information better retained than in its original form.

Abstract or impersonal information is difficult to remember. Use mnemonics to create perception images; they're much, much easier to recall.

There are nine basic types of perception mnemonics: **Music, Name, Expression/Word, Model, Ode/Rhyme, Note Organization, Image, Connection,** and **Spelling.**

Use one of the mnemonics types from the above categories to remember anything. Anything. There's a mnemonic for topics like these:

- Rhymes
- Rules
- Phrases
- Pictures
- Diagrams
- Lists
- Short poems
- Acronyms
- Memorable phrases
- Spelling
- Visual remembrances

CHAPTER 13 MNEMONICS

Outside sources (exteroceptors—the organs responsible for information from outside the body such as the eyes, ears, mouth, and skin).

There's even a mnemonic for spelling the word, *Mnemonics*: "**M**nemonics **N**eatly **E**liminate **M**an's **O**nly **N**emesis– **I**nsufficient **C**erebral **S**torage."

A common mnemonic technique for remembering lists is the creation of an easily remembered acronym. The examples following illustrate the uses of mnemonics in many different societal groups and are great examples of the way mnemonics can be used to aid recall.

Anyone can create their own mnemonics to aid the memorization process. There probably is no sector of society that does not utilize mnemonics to assist in learning or performance. Your personal method doesn't have to be a sentence that creates the triggers for your recall. It can be anything. Really. Anything.

The lists have lots of examples. Look for topics of personal interest (they're alphabetized) and skip the rest.

See Addendum 7 for a list of mnemonic characteristics you can use for development of your personal descriptive mnemonics.

Examples Of Mnemonics Used As Memory Aids

Astronomy
Order of Planets from the Sun: (**M**ercury, **V**enus, **E**arth, **M**ars, **J**upiter, **S**aturn, **U**ranus, **N**eptune, and **P**uto. Note: Pluto has since been reclassified.)

My **V**ery **E**arnest **M**other **J**ust **S**howed **U**s **N**ine **P**lanets

Biology
To remember the lifecycle of cells (**I**nterphase, **P**rophase, **M**etaphase, **A**naphase, **T**elophase, **C**ytokinesis):

I Pee **M**ore **A**fter **T**ea **C**onstantly

To remember the processes that define living things (**M**ovement, **R**espiration, **S**ensation, **G**rowth, **R**eproduction, **E**xcretion, **N**utrition):

MRS. GREN

Business and Economics
To remember the American Institute of CPA's Principles of Professional Conduct: (1. **R**esponsibility 2. The **P**ublic Interest 3. **I**ntegrity 4. **O**bjectivity and Independence 5. **D**ue Care 6. **S**cope and Nature of Services):

Rude **P**enguins **I**rritate **O**ld **D**ying **S**eals

Calendar
A mnemonic for the days of the months is not a rhyme or a jingle but a gestalt. (Gestalt is a set of things, such as a person's thoughts and experiences, which are considered as a whole and regarded as amounting to more than the sum of its parts.)

CHAPTER 13 MNEMONICS

Whereas a traditional mnemonic simply associates the name of the month with the number of days, this one emphasizes the sequence. The 31 and less-than 31-day months would be easy to remember if they simply alternated, but the pattern of month lengths is not that simple. They alternate until the fourth 31-day month, July, which is immediately followed by another 31-day month.

Here's how:

> Since the human hand has four fingers, one can perceive the monthly pattern in a view of the knuckles of two fists, held together. The raised knuckles can be the 31-day months, the dips between them the 30-day-months-and February, and the gap between the hands ignored. (Thus: left-hand-pinky-knuckle = January; dip = February; left-hand-ring-knuckle = March; dip = April, and so on to left-hand-index-knuckle = July; then continue with right-hand-index-knuckle = August; dip = September, etc.).

Chemistry

To remember the series of alkanes (**M**ethane, **E**thane, **P**ropane, **B**utane, **P**entane, **H**exane):

> **M**y **E**normous **P**enguin **B**ounces **P**retty **H**igh

Chronology

To set the clock to accommodate the shift to and from daylight saving time:

> Spring forward, fall back, or
> Spring ahead, fall behind.

To remember the number of days in the months of the year:

> Thirty days hath September, April, June, and November. All the rest have thirty-one, save February, with twenty-eight days clear, and twenty-nine each leap year.

Education

Bloom's Taxonomy is a classification of learning objectives into increasingly broader categories. The objectives are based on shared features (**K**nowledge, **C**omprehension, **A**pplication, **A**nalysis, **S**ynthesis, **E**valuation):

> **K**eep **C**alm **A**t **A**ll **S**porting **E**vents

Engineering

The color code for Resistors: (**B**lack, **B**rown, **R**ed, **O**range, **Y**ellow, **G**reen, **B**lue, **V**iolet, **G**rey, **W**hite, **G**old, **S**ilver):

> **B**ig **B**rown **R**abbits **O**ften **Y**ield **G**reat **B**ig **Vo**cal **G**roans **W**hen **G**ingerly **S**lapped

To remember which way to turn common (right-handed) screws and nuts, including light bulbs:

> Righty tighty, lefty loosey

Geography

To remember the Great Lakes in an arbitrary order:

> **HOMES** (**H**uron, **O**ntario, **M**ichigan, **E**rie, **S**uperior)

To remember the Great Lakes in order of decreasing surface area:

> **S**uper **H**eroes **M**ust **E**at **O**ats. (**S**uperior, **H**uron, **M**ichigan, **E**rie, **O**ntario)

CHAPTER 13 MNEMONICS

To remember the Great Lakes in order from west to east:

Super **M**an **H**elps **E**very **O**ne (**Su**perior, **M**ichigan, **H**uron, **E**rie, **O**ntario)

Geology

The geological periods of the Paleozoic to Cenozoic eras (**Pr**ecambrian, **C**ambrian, **O**rdovician, **S**ilurian, **D**evonian, **C**arboniferous, **P**ermian, **T**riassic, **J**urassic, **C**retaceous):

Pregnant **C**amels **O**rdinarily **S**it **D**own **C**arefully; **P**erhaps **T**heir **J**oints **C**reak

The Mineral Hardness scale 1-10: **T**alc(=1) **G**ypsum(=2) **C**alcite(=3) **F**luorite(=4) **A**patite(=5) **O**rthoclase(=6) **Q**uartz(=7) **T**opaz(=8) **C**orundum(=9) **D**iamond(=10):

Toronto **G**irls **C**an **F**lirt **A**nd **O**nly **Q**uit **T**o **C**hase **D**warves.

For differentiating stalactites and stalagmites:
The 'mites go up and the 'tites come down.

Guitar

The guitar string names in standard tuning from the 6th string to the 1st string (**E,A,D,G,B,E**):

Every **A**dult **D**og **G**rowls **B**arks **E**ats

Conversely, a mnemonic listing the strings in the reverse order (**E,B,G,D,A,E**):

Every **B**eginning **G**uitarist **D**oes **A**ll **E**xercises

History

The first eight U.S. presidents (George **W**ashington, John Quincy **A**dams, Thomas **J**efferson, James **M**adison, James

Monroe, John Quincy **A**dams, Andrew **J**ackson, Martin **V**an Buren):

    Will **A** **J**olly **M**an **M**ake **A** **J**olly **V**isitor?

Law

Seven articles of the United States Constitution (**L**egislative, **E**xecutive, **J**udicial, **S**upremacy, **A**mendment, **S**tatehood, **R**atification):

    Large **E**lephants **J**ump **S**lowly and **S**ink **R**apidly

Math

Order of Operations (**P**arenthesis, **E**xponents, **M**ultiplication, **D**ivision, **A**ddition, **S**ubtraction):

    Please **E**xcuse **M**y **D**ear **A**unt **S**ally

Pi (π):

    May I have a large container of coffee? (The number of letters per word equal Pi's value = 3.1415927)

Medicine

Bones of the wrist (**S**caphoid, **L**unate. **T**riquetral. **P**isiform, **T**rapezium, **T**rapezoid, **C**apitate, **H**amate):

    Some **L**overs **T**ry **P**ositions **T**hat **T**hey **C**an't **H**andle

Onomatology *(the study of proper names of all kinds and the origins of names relating to, connected with, or explaining names)*

Given names (masculine and feminine):

    FrancIs (him) and Frances (her), or Don (son) and Dawn (daughter)

Philosophy

The first 11 (and most important) Ionian philosophers (**T**hales, **H**eraclitus, **E**mpedocles, **P**rotagoras, **L**eucippus, **A**naximander, **Z**eno, **A**naximenes, **P**armenides, **A**naxagoras, **D**emocritus):

THE PLAZA PAD

Physics

To remember rainbow colors in order (**r**ed, **o**range, **y**ellow, **g**reen, **b**lue, **i**ndigo, **v**iolet):

Richard **O**f **Y**ork **G**ave **B**attle **I**n **V**ain

Reading music

Musicians remember the notes associated with the five lines of the treble clef:

Every **G**ood **B**oy **D**oes **F**ine

The four spaces of the treble clef spell out (from the bottom to the top):

Fat **A**lbert **C**an **E**at

Religion

The Twelve Apostles of Jesus (replacing the ancient Hebrew letter "I" with the modern "J"): **B**artholomew, **A**ndrew, **P**hilip, **T**homas, **J**ames, **J**ohn, **J**ames, **J**ude, **J**udas, **S**imon Peter, **S**imon, and **M**atthew):

Remember your **BAPTI^5 S ^{2} M**

To remember the seven deadly sins (**P**ride, **A**varice, **L**ust, **E**nvy, **G**luttony, **A**nger (wrath), **S**loth):

PALE GAS

Spelling

Characteristic sequence of letters:

> I before E, except after C.
>
> Or when sounded "A" as in neighbor, weigh and weight.
>
> Or when sounded like "eye" as in height.
>
> And "weird" is just weird.
>
> Wherever there is a Q there is a U too. (Examples include que, queen, question, quack, quark, quartz, quarry, quit, pique, torque, macaque, and exchequer. However, this statement is violated by some words.)
>
> When two vowels go walking, the first one does the talking. (Examples include oat, eat. The second letter a is silent and the first letter o and e respectively are pronounced.)

Specific syllables in a word:

> **BELIEVE**—"Do not believe a lie."
> **SECRETARY**—"A secretary must keep a secret."
> **TEACHER**—"There is an ache in every teacher."
> **SLAUGHTER**—"Slaughter is laughter with an s at the beginning."
> **SEPARATE**—"Always smell a rat when you spell separate."

Distinguishing between similar words:

> **Complement** and **Compliment:** "Complement adds something to make it enough. Compliment puts you in the limelight."

Principle and **Principal:** "Your principal is your pal."
"A rule can be called a principle."

Stationary and **stationery**: "Stationery contains er and so does paper; stationary (not moving) contains ar and so does car"

Spelling mnemonics:

DIARRHEA—"**D**ining **I**n **A** **R**ough **R**estaurant: **H**urry, **E**xpect **A**ccidents!"

ARITHMETIC—"**A** **R**at **I**n **T**he **H**ouse **M**ay **E**at **T**he **I**ce **C**ream."

MNEMONICS—"**M**nemonics **N**ow **E**rase **M**an's **O**ldest **N**emesis: **I**nsufficient **C**erebral **S**torage."

RHYTHM—"**R**hythm **H**elps **Y**our **T**wo **H**ips **M**ove."

Zoology

A Bactrian camel's back is shaped like the letter B.

A Dromedary camel's back is shaped like the letter D.

Bactrian camel

Dromedary camel

An African elephant's ears are large and shaped like Africa.
An Asian elephant's ears are small and shaped like India.

Information for this chapter came from many authors and Wikipedia.

CHAPTER 14
BUILDING MEMORY SKILLS: A QUICK PREVIEW

This chapter is a short preview of what's coming on the following pages. Consider it a "warm up." Don't skip it!

To take advantage of a really slick memory system—the senior special—you'll have to memorize a very short list of letters and words called "pegs." Peg words will enable you to remember just about everything. The "pegs," which are formed from the phonetic alphabet, are listed in the next chapter. Once you've got the sounds down pat (they're part of the phonetic alphabet), you're off and running!

You'll also want to learn how to convert numbers to consonants (again, using the phonetic alphabet), then to add special letters (mostly vowels) so that you can make words and sentences from the combination. "Chunking" letters and numbers is a big help.

Another way to remember a list of things is to link them together using ridiculous combinations. The link chapter will show you the easy way to do it. Peg words are better...and easier.

Got a topic with a lot of detail in it you want to remember? It's no problem with the Memory Palace. Think of the "palace" as home, sweet home.

Remembering Names and Faces is no big deal (in spite of the problems it creates for you today). The Names and Faces chapter will give you the tools so you will never forget a name again and never forget who the name belongs to!

One of the methods you'll want to learn to use is Substitution and Association. The techniques are a part of just about every memory technique. Replace hard to remember things by substituting for them something that will make the connection stand out and then associate your substitution with the other piece of memory.

Read on.

Get ready to have your whole outlook on memory improved... substantially.

CHAPTER 15
THE PHONETIC ALPHABET, THE KEY TO A BETTER MEMORY!

The phonetic alphabet is used in memory systems to:

Change numbers into rule based alphabetic phonetic sounds that can be converted to words, and

Be an organized list maker, substituting phonetic words for list numbers.

The phonetic alphabet is crucial to memory systems. It consists of 10 paired digits and sounds which can be used to represent any number. Practice converting numbers to a phonetic sound. There is a hidden benefit in doing this: the conversion of numbers to unique sounds forces awareness and contributes to concentration.

The following table shows it all. It may not make sense at this point; it'll fit together soon.

The digit	will always be this sound	Memory Aid	Phonetic Peg Word
0	z, s, soft c	First sound of the word, "zero".	zee
1	t or d	The letter t has one down stroke	tie
2	n	Typewritten n has two down strokes.	Noah
3	m	Typewritten m has three down strokes.	ma
4	r	The word four, ends with an r.	rye
5	l	Roman numeral for 50 is L.	law
6	j, sh, ch, soft g	The letter J turned around is almost like the number 6.	shoe
7	k, hard c, hard g	Two sevens can form a lowercase "k."	cow
8	f, v, ph	Written f and the figure 8 both have two loops.	ivy
9	b, p	The number 9 turned around is P.	bee
10	t or d and s	"T" and "s" combine to make "10."	Toes
	a, e, i, o, u, w, h, y, x	These are the "neutral" letters.	

CHAPTER 15 THE PHONETIC ALPHABET, THE KEY TO A BETTER MEMORY!

Other that what you see above, there are a few additional rules:

Vowels do not have any meaning. They are merely used as convenient fillers when you translate between numbers and words.

Double letter combinations are only counted as one consonant sound. For example the word 'ladder' translates as l, d, and r (only one 'd' is used).

Silent letters are not counted.

Certain consonant sounds are not used in the phonetic alphabet and they, too, are used as fillers. They are W, H, Y, and X. There is an easy rule to remember these four extra filler letters. Just ask the question, "Why x?"

The easy-to-use peg words were developed by Harry Lorayne and Jerry Lucas. Other systems use different peg words. If you're interested in other choices, see Addendum 1. For more detailed information, Google "Memory Systems," or any of the authors mentioned in Addendum 2.

CHAPTER 16
REMEMBER EVERY NUMBER

The information in this chapter will make you a memory expert!

'Want to easily remember numbers? Imagine grouping several numbers together, then converting them to descriptive letters. Next, add some non-counting letters to the grouping so that the combinations become easily remembered words.

Sounds great, doesn't it!

If there are lots of numbers to be remembered and to make it even easier to remember your letter-words, link the word groupings together into bizarre, outlandish, wild and crazy combinations that are easily visualized.

When you want to get back to your numbers, simply eliminate the non-counting letters and then convert the remaining letters to their numerical counterpart.

Call the letters that are representations of numbers phonetic alphabetic consonants. They don't change…ever. (See the chart following). The non-counting letters are a, e, i, o, u, w, h, y, and x. Use them anywhere and as often as you wish. They are the fillers that make the real letters (the ones that represent your numbers) work.

Start by looking at the table on the next page.

CHAPTER 16 REMEMBER EVERY NUMBER

Here are the first 10-digits and their alphabetic equivalents that are the keys to easy alpha for number conversion. This list is part of the "Consonant Peg List." (Missing are the "Peg words; more about that later.)

The Digit	Alphabetic Representation
0	z, s, soft c
1	t or d
2	n
3	m
4	r
5	L
6	j, sh, ch, soft g
7	k, hard c, hard g
8	f, v, ph
9	b, p
10	t or d and s
	a, e, i, o, u, w, h, y, x

Alphabetic representations could go as high as needed, and each number would be unique.

Here's a great example of how the conversion process works:

Start with this number: **9185271952163909211 2** (Don't worry, this is an example that's already been worked out!)

Using the chart from the previous page, the numbers convert to these phonetic letters: **btflnkdblndjmpspnddn.** Then add **non-counting** letters as required to make words, (These are the non-counting letters actually used: aeauiuaeouuaow.)

The converted string of counting and non-counting letters becomes **"A Beautiful Naked Blond Jumps Up and Down."**

Making this conversion is pretty impressive and not something you'd want to tackle right now. Maybe later. However, I don't think you'll have any trouble making a picture of those words!

It's not likely you'll be challenged to convert a long string of numbers like 91852719521639092112 on a daily basis. But credit cards, drivers' licenses, telephone numbers, and passwords? Can you remember their numbers?

The 10 digit Consonant Peg List and the phonetic letter equivalents are the keys to easy number-to-alpha conversion and memory retention. Peg Number conversion is a powerful, easy-to-use technique.

It's the best memory system for seniors.

You **must** learn the "peg" letter(s) for each number. Learn to convert numbers to their Phonetic alpha equivalent, and then add some non-counting letters so that the result is a word. It becomes easy to do after a while.

Returning the converted words back to the original numbers: just drop the non-counting letters and match the remaining consonants to their equivalent numbers.

For convenience, break large numbers into groups of 3 or 4

letters as was done above ("chunking"), and create words from those letters by adding non-counting letters.

For example, **9185** of the *91852719521639092112* was separated from the whole set and was converted to ***btfl***. With the addition of the non-counting letters, ***eauiu, btfl*** became **"beautiful."**

Likewise, **271** (the next three letters) became the group, **nkd.** The three numbers (now converted to **nkd**) then became naked when the non-counting letters ae were added. Link words together by creating a picture you can easily remember.

Our brains are notoriously poor at memorizing numbers. The reason is numbers are abstract concepts. Although they are represented visually by symbols, they don't feel very real or appealing to our brains. As has been written many times, our brains work best using lively, vibrant images. Numbers don't qualify. Converting numbers to phonetic letters is the beginning of a process transforming abstract, dull numbers into vivid, striking images. When we do that, committing numbers to memory is a snap!

If you haven't already done so, memorize now the letters and sounds in the peg list. It will only take a few minutes.

Make pictures out of numbers

The heart of the process—and the key to converting numbers to images and vice-versa—is the 10-item mnemonic table, the peg list.

The table on page 111 shows the corresponding alpha letters for the digits 0-9. The alpha letters, when combined with vowels and neutral letters, form words.

As a practical example, take the number 42. According to the table, the digits in the number 42 translate to r and n. Form a word with r and n by adding neutral letters (from the last row of the table: a, e, i, o, u, w, h, y, and x). The word "rain" is an easy result: add a and i to rn (42).

Decoding a word back to numbers is straightforward. "Mouse," for instance, becomes 30 (drop the non-counting letters o,u,e, leaving m and s. M is 3 and s becomes 0.

The conversion process may seem a little slow and cumbersome at first, but with just a little bit of practice, it becomes second nature.

There are just a couple more notes to bear in mind:

> Number conversions are strictly phonetic. That means the replacement images are based on how the words sound, not how they're spelled. If a word has double letters that account for just one sound, count only one sound (for example, the r sound in cherry counts as only one number). By the same token, mute letters (such as the b in debt) should be ignored.

> When coming up with words, choose those that are easy to visualize. Concrete nouns, such as objects or animals, always work better than abstract nouns, adjectives, or verbs. (There are other rules, too. Don't worry about them. For our purposes, just remember these.)

CHAPTER 16 REMEMBER EVERY NUMBER

To summarize: every number has a consonant alphabetic partner (1="t"). From the numbers, take their representative letters and make words by adding non-counting letters. Every word you create should be very visual—the more outlandish the better.

You don't have to do a whole long number as one grouping. Chunk it. That means break a long number down into groups. From each group of numbers, create the alpha representation. For instance, 123 is tnm or dnm (these are the consonants). Make a word with the consonants by adding neutral letters (a, e, i, o, u, w, h, y, and x). Here are some words that can be created: autonomy (tnm), denim (*dnm*), dynamo (*dnm*), pseudonym (*dnm*).

From the second group, add non-counting letters to the consonants and make a word. Do the same for the next group. Then LINK the words. Do the same for all the digits. The words you've formed represent all the digits and should be something outlandish that stands out in your mind.

If you used four groups of three consonants, you know a 12-digit number. Drop the non-counting letters, transpose the consonants to digits, and you've got your number back. You can do it forward and backward. You've turned intangible numbers into tangibles!

Remember 918527195216390092112? ...No? How about "a beautiful naked blonde jumps up and down?" The process works!

The only caveat: the letters must go into the word in the same sequence as the numbers appear in the whole number. To do otherwise would change the numerical presentation when converting the words back to the original numbers.

Converting numbers to words is not easy, even with the free letters. However, there is a shortcut that will make the process much easier. The website, www.phoneticmnemonic.com will take the numbers from a group and spit out a list of words.

Following are the results of using the software to create words from a telephone number 281-941-4952. The process starts by breaking the numbers into three groups. What you'll see are the words the software created.

281(nvd)= Envied, innovate, invade, invite, naiveté, neophyte, nevada, nifty, sniffed, snuffed, unfit, unified.

941(prt)= Abhorred, aboard, abort, abroad, apart, appeared, aspirate, aspired, bard, bared, barred, beard, berate, beret, berth, bird, birth, board, bored, borrowed, brad, braid, brat, bread, breath, breathe, breathy, bred, breed, brewed, bride, bright, broad, brood, broth, brought, brute, buried, hybrid, operate, paired, parade, pared, parity, parody, parried, parrot, part, party, peered, period, pert, pirate, pored, port, poured, powered, prayed, pretty, preyed, pride, pried, prod, proud, puerto, purdue, purity, seaport, separate, sobered, spared, sparred, spirit, sport, sprayed, spread, sprite, sprout, spurred, spurt, support, upright, uproot, upward, whispered, zippered

4952(rbln)= Airplane, rebellion

CHAPTER 16 REMEMBER EVERY NUMBER

Select a word from the possible combinations:

For 281 choose **invade (2=n; 8=v; 1=d)**
For 941 choose **pirate (9=p; 4=r; 1=t)**
For 4952 choose **rebellion (4=r; 9=b; ll=5; 2=n)**

Link the three words, invade, pirate, and rebellion together to create a memorable and exaggerated scene.

The result might be a large group of red-coated soldiers who decide to (**invade**) the (**pirate**) stronghold to put down the (**rebellion**). The pirates all have full beards, bright headbands, knives in their mouths, and are wielding large swords.

Link the crazy picture to the owner of the telephone number and you've got the number locked forever in your memory.

Whenever you think of the person, that outlandish scene flashes through your mind and you remember the phone number: 281-941-4952.

It works!

CHAPTER 17
VISUALIZATION AND ASSOCIATION

Primitive families had no spoken language. They communicated by making noises and waving their arms around, dancing little jigs, and stuff like that. The reason they are being mentioned is because of the language they didn't speak.

During their lifetimes, physically moving around, grunts, nods and unintelligible sounds had to convey to others thoughts or action needs. They had one other tool available: pictures. A stick and a clear patch of ground was probably their best communication method.

Want your caveman buddy to go hunting with you? Draw a spear and an animal image, look into his eyes, and watch for the blink or nod that says, "Yes."

You can imagine the pictures cave men and women drew on the ground or walls of their caves—all a part of their communication system, along with grunts, head shaking and arm waving. Visual images were their lifeline.

Association

Today, the picture in our head is still the way we effectively communicate. If we can create a visual image that someone else can also see in his or her mind, we are most able to make a point. And we add new information by associating the new image with something already in our heads.

Memorization occurs only when two images are associated. As you will learn, the peg number 2 is only usable when it is associated with an image (2=Noah). What comes to mind when

CHAPTER 17 VISUALIZATION AND ASSOCIATION

you see or hear the word, Noah? (A bearded man guiding animals into the ark?) When a memory already in the long-term section of your brain is associated with a new memory, the new memory becomes recallable. Images must be joined. Side-by-side doesn't work. To be certain the new data is recallable, integrate (join) the images together in the most bizarre, graphic way you can think of.

Visualization

Joining images together in an outlandish manner is called visualization. It is an essential part of the memory process. Retrievable memory only occurs when a new visual image is associated with another image already stored in the brain. Successfully linked (associated) to a peg, the new data is retrievable and usable. Interaction has occurred.

The visualization process is a memory enhancer:

    Images are easier to remember than facts

    Creating images forces you to focus ("Original Awareness")

    Reviewing images reinforces your memory

The images you create don't need to be complicated, but they do need to be clear about what is being represented. The more clearly you visualize the image, the better the image will act as a "hook" to retrieve information from memory.

The larger, more incredible, sillier, or more outrageous the images, the better they will work as mental hooks. That's because your mind remembers the unusual far better than the ordinary.

With experience, the mental conversion process is very fast. Images literally flash one after the other in your mind's eye, as you instantly choose an image that will represent your fact.

Interaction

Interaction is the association of two items and the creation of a connection between them. One of the images must be interacting with the other image. Side by side images do not count; there must be interaction. When the two images are combined (joined) as a unit, each part of the unit serves as a cue to remember the rest of the unit.

When visual images are clear, distinct, and strong, there is a good probability the visualized images are effectively associated and interacting, and thereby recallable. You won't forget!

Here are some ways to create a retrievable image:

> **Make the image vivid.**
>
> **Create a clear mental picture.**
>
> **Add a lot of detail** to the image.
>
> See the **image in motion.**
>
> **Substitute.** See one item in place of the other. Substitution enhances the probability of remembering.
>
> **Exaggerate.** Exaggeration is an important way to associate a new thought to an existing one.
>
> **Familiarize.** Associate the new image with prior experiences. Familiarity increases the probability of recall.

CHAPTER 17 VISUALIZATION AND ASSOCIATION

Make the created image bizarre. Imagery is another tool for associating new information to already existing information.

In summary, if you want to remember a new piece of information, visualize and associate it with something you already know or remember, using one of the ways above. It's best if the association is done in a way that is highly unusual or ridiculous.

Once you've got your new information irretrievably attached to known data, you can use it. Making it one item in a list of items utilizes the "consonant peg word" memory system. Peg words convert numbers to a visual image that you can associate (or link) with your new information. Once the visual image is in your mind, (converted), next is the association (linking) of the image to a peg word that's part of a numerical sequence. Do that and you'll be able to recall any item by its sequence in the list or by the image itself and its place in the sequence.

The Peg Word/Number Memory System is unique in that peg words relate to the remembered item or the remembered item relates back to its peg word. You'll learn how in the next chapter.

Images are concrete, while raw information is often abstract. Visualization and association are the way to convert abstract information into easy-to-remember mental pictures. Linked to your number pegs, the images become mental hooks that allow you to retrieve information from your long-term memory in any sequence. Linked to an existing memory, new and old data are combined and the memory is retrievable.

To remember anything, you are forced to concentrate and use repetition as a memory aid. Converting a fact to a mental image forces you to actively focus on the information as you change facts to images. The process enables you to become more aware of what you're learning. Harry Lorayne calls this "Original Awareness."

Some scientists believe we never forget anything. Nine times out of ten, the reason we can't remember is that we can't find the information in our brains. It's there; we just can't get to it. We have not made it a habit to create the mental hooks (the visualizations) that we need to grab and pull out the information. With practice, you'll get very good at the visualization and association memory technique, and be able to create mental hooks for anything you want to remember.

That's using your brain in the right way.

Visualization and association are techniques of memory professionals.

It works. Make it your technique, too

CHAPTER 18
THE CONSONANT-NUMBER PEG SYSTEM

The three major memory systems are Peg, Memory Palace, and Link. Each has a value depending on your activity. I suspect peg word lists will be the most valuable and most used technique for seniors. Work on developing a proficiency with peg words first.

We're beginning to repeat some information as the methodology starts to come together. Peg lists are a great, easy way to remember anything in numerical sequence.

At the heart of a peg list are consonant letters which represent numbers. You were introduced to this conversion process in Chapter 15 with an explanation of the phonetic alphabet. (Remember: Phonetics are a way to represent the sounds of human speech in writing, often with special symbols or unconventional spelling.)

The peg list process starts by converting a digit to a phonetic-equivalent consonant (for example, 1=t). Then non-counting letters (always either a, e, i, o, u, w, h, y, or x) are added to the consonant so that the result is an easily pictured word. For example, 7=cow; "c" is the consonant equivalent for 7 and "ow" are the non-counting letters added to make the word visual. The peg word, cow, which was made by combining consonants and non-counting letters, is a mnemonic memory aid to help recall the number the word represents. To get back to the peg number, non-counting consonants (o and w) are dropped, leaving only the letter (c) that represent a number (c=7). The combination of the list number and the word to be remembered as that number are a part of the "Consonant-Number" peg list.

Here's how: Say you have a list of things to do today. The third item on your list is to purchase a screwdriver. The peg number for three is "ma." Associate a picture of your mother using a huge screwdriver to repair a cash register in your local Home Depot. Then when you wonder what was the third item on your list, remember that 3 is represented by ma. What's the picture that comes to your mind? Of course: your mother and the screwdriver.

The process is not difficult.

Although this example is relatively simple, the technique is usable in any situation. Visualization and association take advantage of an amazing fact about human memory: most people remember images better than verbal or written information. When you remember an event from your past, it's a series of pictures, not words, that come to mind.

To repeat, following are the 10 phonetic peg words that are key to remembering everything in every list:

The digit	will always be this sound	Memory Aid	Phonetic Peg Word
1	t or d	The letter t has one down stroke.	tie
2	n	Typewritten n has two down strokes.	Noah
3	m	Typewritten m has three down strokes.	ma

CHAPTER 18 THE CONSONANT-NUMBER PEG SYSTEM

4	r	The word four ends with an r.	rye
5	l	Roman numeral for 50 is L	law
6	j, sh, ch, soft g	The letter J turned around is almost like the number 6.	shoe
7	k, hard c, hard g	Two sevens can form a lowercase "k."	cow
8	f, v, ph	Written f and the figure 8 both have two loops	ivy
9	b, p	The number 9. turned 180° is b	bee
0	z, s, soft c	First sound of the word, "zero".	zee
	a, e, i, o, u, w, h, y, x	The neutral, non-counting letters	

You should memorize the peg words and the digits they represent (if you haven't already done that). Once you've got the 10 peg words down pat, when you want to remember anything in a list, associate a ridiculous image of what you want to remember with a peg word image and you've got both the sequence and the item captured. Link as many words as you want.

To review: the peg list system eliminates the stress of remembering items in numerical order. The peg list becomes a filing cabinet in your mind that enables you to access data in any order. It begins when a phonetic-sound letter becomes a substitute for a number. Next, non-counting letters are added to the letter-for-number so that the result is an easily pictured word. Numbers above 10 combine the phonetic sounds from the first 10 numbers to create two digit numbers.

It's not nearly as complicated as it sounds.

The value of peg word memory systems is that by converting numbers to words, the words can then be associated to something you want to remember. The system takes information you already know well (numbers and letters) and associates them with the new facts you want to remember. This is a very good system for seniors.

Numbers are abstract and hard to visualize. However, because you will never forget how to count, associating information with numbers creates a dependable mental sequential filing system. The peg system solves the visualization problem by making abstract numbers and letters concrete and visual. Peg systems remind you of what you are supposed to remember. If you're looking for a big advantage over rote memorization, this is it. Every number has a sound; create a peg word for it, associate an image you can easily remember to it, and BANG, you've got the item in your list in a specific order that is easily recallable.

By creating a word/number list, peg systems allow direct retrieval in any sequence. This is important information! For example, if you were working with a difficult topic like the cranial nerves, with numerical pegs you can immediately say, "The Trigeminal Nerve is the fifth cranial nerve." You can do this because you previously had associated "law" (the phonetic

CHAPTER 18 THE CONSONANT-NUMBER PEG SYSTEM

representation of 5) with the words, "Trigeminal Nerve" (perhaps by visualizing a big judge holding his huge book of laws open to the page defining the function of the Trigeminal Nerve).

Pegs can be used repeatedly. Rename your list and start over as if nothing had happened.

An incredible truth about the brain is that it can distinguish between the same numerical list (i.e., the same pegs) being used multiple times for different information. For example, one memory systems research study showed that normal people were able to memorize six different lists of items at the same time using the same pegs.

Other memory systems, like Link and Memory Palace, also tie information together effectively. But they cannot be used to recall a particular item directly, like the information at the third from the end of your Peg list. With those systems, you must mentally run through the entire link to get to the item you want. Not so with pegs. You can immediately go to the word on your list you associated to it, whether it was the fifth or seventh or ninety-first, by remembering the number assigned.

As an example, suppose you want to buy a 30-Watt light bulb, the seventh item (cow) on your list of things you want to get at the supermarket.

Here's how: combine the image for the bulb and the encoded image for 30 using the mnemonic table. 30 translates to the letters m and s and converts to mouse. Mouse in a light bulb is a good picture that represents what is wanted, a 30-watt light bulb.

The task, then, is to create a mental picture combining light bulb, mouse, and cow. The secret for this to work is to make the mental picture memorable. Make it crazy, ridiculous, offensive, unusual, animated, and nonsensical. In short, make it fun!

What's the zaniest way to combine light bulb with mouse and cow? Here's an example:

> I'm in my local supermarket, in the electrical accessories aisle. As I pass the light bulbs section… Pow! A bulb breaks and a cow jumps out! A light bulb became a cow. I remember: a light bulb is the seventh item on my peg grocery list (cow= 7).
>
> Then, even more strange, a mouse starts coming out of the cow's udders instead of milk! 'Mouse' converts to the counting letters, m and s. M and s represent 30. 30 watts. The mouse runs away, squeaking frantically.

Imagine that scene vividly in your mind and try not remembering that 30-watt mouse and cow the next time you're in that supermarket aisle.

Here's another example: You want to remember a list of 10 things. Your ninth item is pillow. Associate that to bee, your peg word for nine. Imagine pillows, instead of bees, swarming all over you and stinging you. Crazy enough?

What about a really big list? Everyone can remember a small list. The great thing about the system is that you can easily combine it with other phonetic words to make as many list numbers as you wish. That's what makes the system scalable and able to handle many items.

CHAPTER 18 THE CONSONANT-NUMBER PEG SYSTEM

For memorizing multiple items with one number, create a mental scene combining the phonetic peg word number and your images linked, forming a sequence. (The Memory Palace uses this method.)

The association of a peg number with something else by making a combination that is a wild, wild picture, is very powerful. You can remember anything this way. Your challenge is the creation of a vivid, crazy image that reminds you of what you want to remember.

There is no limit to the number of digit/sounds that can be combined. The previous steps are the basic tools you need to use the system. To make it more powerful and efficient, use a predefined image list for the list numbers 1 to 100. This will greatly improve your speed when forming images since you won't need to imagine different words each time you use the numbers.

On the next page is a 1 to 100 peg list. The list was developed by Harry Lorayne and Jerry Lucas.

100 Peg Words

1	tie	21	net	41	rod	61	sheet	81	fit
2	Noah	22	nun	42	rain	62	chain	82	phone
3	ma	23	name	43	ram	63	chum	83	foam
4	rye	24	Nero	44	rower	64	cherry	84	fur
5	law	25	nail	45	roll	65	jail	85	file
6	shoe	26	notch	46	roach	66	cho choo	86	fish
7	cow	27	neck	47	rock	67	chalk	87	fog
8	ivy	28	knife	48	roof	68	chef	88	fife
9	bee	29	knob	49	rope	69	ship	89	bob
10	toes	30	mouse	50	lace	70	case	90	bus
11	tot	31	mat	51	lot	71	cot	91	bat
12	tin	32	moon	52	lion	72	coin	92	bone
13	tomb	33	mummy	53	loom	73	comb	93	bum
14	tire	34	mower	54	lure	74	car	94	bear
15	towel	35	mule	55	lily	75	coal	95	bell
16	dish	36	match	56	leech	76	cage	96	beach
17	tack	37	mug	57	log	77	coke	97	nook
18	dove	38	movie	58	lava	78	cave	98	puff
19	tub	39	mop	59	lip	79	cob	99	pipe
20	nose	40	rose	60	cheese	80	fuzz	100	disease

Of course, memorizing 100 mnemonics requires a lot of time and effort, but once it's all in your long-term memory, you can use it for life. To be fair, you don't need to memorize it (in the traditional sense of the word). Just start using the mnemonics; the images will soon come to you.

The basic peg list can be used over and over. The list can also be linked to other memory systems, like the Memory

CHAPTER 18 THE CONSONANT-NUMBER PEG SYSTEM

Palace. A "peg" is just a mental hook on which you hang other information. The hook acts as a reminder to help you mentally retrieve information. Associate a piece of information with a number; then simply thinking of the number will give you back the information.

Want to remember the amendments to the constitution? The seventh amendment gives citizens the right to trial by jury. See yourself in a courtroom being judged by a jury of cows.

To remind you that the 13th amendment abolished slavery, picture a tomb (13) being a slave driver.

Who was the 15th president? Imagine a blue cannon (Buchanan) firing a towel (15) instead of a cannon ball.

To remember Bible verses, using John 14:27 as an example: "Peace I leave with you, my peace I give unto you: not as the world giveth, give I unto you. Let not your heart be troubled, neither let it be afraid." Here's how: Start by making a visual image of the numbers 14 and 27. (14 = "tire"; "t" = 1, "r" = 4); (27 = "neck"; "n" = 2, "ck" = 7).

Then create a visual image that links the numbers together: imagine the words of peace being spoken to your friend John right before he enters a contest for swinging a tire around his neck hula hoop style. (This unusual image is odd enough that you should remember it!)

The beauty of this system is that you will be able to recite any item and its number in the list just by referring to the item or its number.

The Phonetic Peg System is based on the Phonetic Alphabet and is designed to accommodate large lists of items. Ten basic consonant sounds are related to the 10 numerical digits 0-9.

Vowels, silent letters, double letter combinations, and the consonants W, H, Y and X are not used in the alphabet, but can be used as filler letters when forming words.

The Phonetic Peg Words transpose to their corresponding numerical values.

It's OK to use linking to reinforce the peg words.

Items to be remembered are associated to the peg words in wild and crazy ways.

In the digit and consonant list on the next page, help yourself to reinforce your knowledge of the first 10 peg words. Write a peg word for the digits. Use counting consonants and as many of the free letters you want.

Don't forget the free letters!

free   a, e, i, o, u, w, h, y, x

Digit	Consonant	Peg Word
1	d	
1	t	
1	h	
2	n	
3	m	
4	r	
5	l	
6	j	
6	sh	
6	ch	
6	soft g	
7	k	
7	hard c	
7	hard g	
8	v	
8	f	
9	b	
10	p	
10	s	
10	z	
10	soft c	
free	a, e, i, o, u, w, h, y, x	

CHAPTER 19
CHUNKING

Our brains will only retain information if it's fed in a certain way. Most of us cannot remember things if we try to soak in too much at one time. In 1956, psychologist George A. Miller came up with the concept that our brains can't handle memorizing things in lists bigger than five to nine items. His study on short-term memory was called "The Magical Number Seven, Plus or Minus Two." Other scientists seem to agree there is a limit to the number of items we can recall.

The conclusion of his study was that to remember best and and easiest, long lists should be broken down into manageable "chunks."

Of course you can remember lists longer than seven items. But be smart. It's easier to remember a long list of items if the list is broken down into manageable chunks. Remembering short lists is relatively easy. Once done, our brains are able to put the chunks of lists together for one big long list.

How to Chunk

Suppose you needed to purchase the following list of 12 grocery items (and you happened not to have pen and paper handy and you've consciously chosen not to use a peg list): spring water, sponges, apples, dish washing liquid, coffee, tangerines, lemonade, laundry detergent, grapes, milk, limes, and paper towels. It would be difficult to remember 12 different items over the 20 minutes you needed to drive to the supermarket.

But you can. Here's how: "Chunk" them into three subgroups, fruit (apples, tangerines, grapes, limes), beverages (spring water, coffee, lemonade, milk), and household cleaning supplies

CHAPTER 19 CHUNKING

(sponges, dish washing liquid, laundry detergent, paper towels). The information will be much more manageable because you've essentially reduced twelve items to three, using each sub-category as a link to its four members.

Here's another grocery list. Try memorizing it:

Egg	Butter
Flour	Syrup
Milk	Cereal
Bacon	Blueberries
Baking powder	

Not so easy? There are nine items in this list. Most of us would have difficulty remembering all of them. However, "chunk" them into needed ingredients lists for three different breakfast menus and it's a piece of cake. Here's how:

Day one: Eggs and bacon.

Day two: Pancakes, requiring flour, baking powder, milk, syrup, and butter.

Day three: Cereal, milk, blueberries (it doesn't hurt anything to repeat milk).

Try it now! Chances are, you can remember every item. Why? You've "tricked" your brain into thinking there are only three things to remember (eggs, pancakes, and cereal) instead of nine. The ingredients are linked to each heading.

Easy!

Chunking can also be used to divide a large sequence of items into several shorter sequences Remember the *"beautiful naked blond?"*

If you're again caught without pen and paper as someone is giving you a ten-digit phone number, rely on the usual three-three-four subgrouping of digits. The number 6178714902 is tough to recall; 617-871-4902 is easier.

Use Chunking to Cram Information

When you think of all the information you have to study when you've got important information to absorb, you can easily become overwhelmed. Use chunking as the first step to storing the information into your short-term memory.

How? Reduce the information into categories. Boil all the information down to five-to-nine big categories and write them down.

Here's how:

1. Gather all your notes and texts in one place.
2. Identify the important terms. Go back through the text and your notes to identify all the important words or phrases. There may be dozens of important terms. Highlight and write them down.
3. Write a short definition for each term.
4. Identify five to nine important concepts and write them down. These are the main ideas you need to understand the topic. Use a separate note card for each concept. (Concepts are usually chapter titles; decide which the really important ones are.)
5. Write a short paragraph in your own words that define or discuss each major concept. Include several of the important terms in your writing.

CHAPTER 19 CHUNKING

6. Go back and forth, reading and testing yourself on the individual terms and the definitions until you are comfortable.
7. Test yourself with fresh, blank note cards. Re-write the main ideas and try reproducing your definitions without looking at your previous cards. Each time you include one of the terms, highlight it or underline it. This is a visual procedure that will reinforce information.
8. Repeat step 7 until you can incorporate all your terms into your concept paragraphs.

By using this method, you are chunking all of the important terms into major concepts.

To review, here's how you chunk textual information:

Identify important terms; write a definition of each in your own words.

Identify the five-to-nine essential concepts (the chunk words). Write about each concept in your own words. Use appropriate terms.

Test yourself on the terms and concepts; repeat until you can do them all.

Write (from memory) your understanding of the concepts and terms. Keep doing it until you can recall the concepts and all the terms with little or no coaching.

Finally, use every technique you've learned to get the information stored in your brain: association, substitution, link, peg words, memory palace, and visualization.

CHAPTER 20
LINKING

The Link System is used to remember things in sequence. Remember this word: "sequence."

Linking is one way to remember speeches, formulas, numbers, reading material, poems, technical articles, lists, lyrics, and stories. (Linking numbers is covered later in this chapter.)

Here's how:

> 1. Start by imagining a silly, memorable image that represents the type of list you want to remember. Include in this image the first item on your list. This image is your list header.
>
> 2. Think of another silly, memorable image that links the first item on the list to the second item.
>
> 3. Think of a new image that links the second item to the third item.
>
> 4. Think of an image that links the third item to the fourth item.

Continue in this way, creating mental images for the remaining items in the list.

It's important to make your links crazy or memorable in some way. For each subsequent link, associate the previous image with the next. Each link reminds you of the next item. There is no limit to the number of links you can create in this manner.

Here is an example of using the Link System to remember the counties in the South of England (Avon, Dorset, Somerset, Cornwall, Wiltshire, Devon, Gloucestershire, Hampshire, and

CHAPTER 20 LINKING

Surrey), certainly not names you would have had a reason to know in the past.

Start by imagining a map showing South England. Then, picture in the most outlandish imagery you can create:

> An AVON (Avon) lady shouting "Avon calling" and knocking on a heavy oak DOoR (Dorset).
>
> The DOoR opens to show a beautiful SuMmER landscape with a SETting sun (Somerset).
>
> The setting sun shines down on a field of CORN (Cornwall).
>
> The CORN is so dry it is beginning to WILT (Wiltshire).
>
> The WILTing corn stalks slowly droop onto the tail of a sleeping DEVil (Devon).
>
> On the DEVil's horn is a GLOSsy (Gloucestershire) HAM (Hampshire) which he got when a woman hit him over the head with it.
>
> In pain, the Devil now feels SORRY (Surrey) he bothered her.

There is no need to be any reason or underlying plot to the sequence of images. Only the images and the links between images are important. Although learning the Link technique is uncomplicated, it is easy to confuse the order of, or forget, images from a sequence.

Here's a way to link numbers:

Create words of the numbers (using the phonetic alphabet that's a part of your Peg List) and then Link together the words you create. (It's not always necessary to make the phonetic sounds of a long number form a sentence in order to remember the number; linking is an option.)

Want to remember your driver's license number (941140)? For a series of numbers, chunk to make groups of numbers into words and then link your number/words to one another.

Here's how:

Phonetically convert the numbers 941: *The 9 is p or b, the 4 is r, and the 1 is t, d, or h. Add enough letters that don't count to the p,r,t, and make a word you can visualize out of them, like parrot (two consonants count as one). You could also have made words like bread, proud, apart, berate, brat, board, or bored. Choose* **parrot.**

The next set of numbers, 140, converts (*1 is d or t; 4 is r, and 0 is s*) to words like duress, tears, throws, dress. *Choose* **dress**.

Link the words. Imagine a huge, very colorful **parrot** wearing an orange frilly **dress.**

Converting the numbers 941140 to phonetic alphabet letters, then into words, and then linking the results, captures six digits. You could, just as easily, have captured nine or 12, or 20 digits. You've taken abstract, intangible numbers and made silly, big, and colorful pictures out of them! Pictures you can remember. You've easily linked them together. Your objective was to make the images you created in your mind so ridiculous they jump out!

You did!

What's your license number? Convert the numbers into an image like that orange-dressed parrot and you've got it. (The

CHAPTER 20 LINKING

way to convert numbers containing both letters and numbers is covered in Chapter 26, "Remember License Plates.")

In summary, here are the ways to link a combination of numbers or words together to make a ridiculous image:

Substitute. Picture one item instead of another.

Out of proportion. Make your items larger than life.

Exaggerate. Make any number excessive; see "millions" instead of one.

Action. If you can, make your action physical. Imagine things flying, or charging at you, or hitting you.

The subject you're remembering starts the link ("What's my license number?"). Then link unusual, unbelievable, ridiculous, out of the ordinary, novel, or marvelous images to it. Repeat the process as long as necessary. After a while, you won't need the image.

Don't under estimate the difficulty of creating bizarre images. It's also difficult linking one picture to another. With practice it gets easier. Linking works!

However, there are three limitations to the link system:

There is no numerical order imposed when memorizing. This makes it difficult to determine the numerical position of an item.

If any item is forgotten, the entire list may be in jeopardy.

There is the potential for confusing repeated segments of the list, a common problem when memorizing binary digits.

Linking can use mnemonic sentence structure to help recall a list Remember "Will A Jolly Man Make A Jolly Visitor?" Mnemonic words linked together made an easy list of the first eight U.S. presidents (George Washington, John Adams, Thomas Jefferson, James Madison, James Monroe, John Quincy Adams, Andrew Jackson, and Martin Van Buren).

In Summary

Linking may be the way you choose to work through long topics with lots of terms. Evaluate the merits of linking as compared to peg lists, and choose the technique that works best for you. Seniors will probably find the peg list is easiest.

CHAPTER 21
THE MEMORY PALACE

What's coming next is a great way to remember a lot of information for a speech or presentation.

The technique is effective and fun to use. And it's not hard to learn. Associating physical locations with mental images is a powerful memory combination.

A version of the system has been used since ancient Rome, and has been credited with some incredible memory feats. Memory professionals use different names for the concept (such as "The Journey" or "Method of Loci."), but the process is the same.

Using his own version of The Journey, eight-time world memory champion Dominic O'Brien was able to memorize 54 decks of cards in sequence (that's 2,808 cards!), viewing each card only once.

And there are countless other similar achievements attributed to people using the technique or variations of it. Even in fiction, there are several references to the technique. In Thomas Harris' novel, *Hannibal*, for example, serial killer Hannibal Lecter uses The Memory Palace method to store amazingly vivid memories of years of intricate patient records (sadly, that scene was left out of the movie).

The concept has earned a place in everyday vocabulary. We say, "in the first place," "in the second place," etc.

Of course, most of us are not in Dominic's memory championship line of business (or in Hannibal's, for that matter!). But the method is amazingly effective in all kinds of endeavors, such as a presentation you're about to deliver, learning a foreign language, preparing for a book review, a Bible chapter discussion, and many others. It can even be used to jog your memory.

The Memory Palace five-step technique is based on the fact that we're extremely good at remembering places we know. The term is a metaphor for any well-known place you're able to easily visualize. It can be the inside of your home, or the route you take every day to work. A familiar place becomes your place to store and recall any kind of information. For most of us, our home is our palace!

Here's how:

1. Choose Your Memory Palace

Pick a place you're very familiar with. The effectiveness of the technique relies on your ability to mentally see and walk around in that place with ease. You should be able to be there at will, using only your mind's eye.

A good first choice would be your own home. The more vividly you can visualize that place's details, the more effective your memorization will be.

Define a specific route within your palace. Don't just visualize a static scene. Instead of simply picturing your home, imagine a specific detailed walk through. This makes the technique much more powerful, as you'll be able to recall items in a specific order.

There are other place and route options, such as a walk through your neighborhood, but for most of us, we're most familiar with our homes.

2. List Distinctive Features

Pay attention to specific features in the place you chose. For example, if you picked a walk through your home, the first noticeable feature would probably be the front door.

Next, mentally walk into your Memory Palace. After you go through the door, what's in the first room?

Analyze the room methodically. It's best if you establish a standard procedure, such as always looking from left to right. What is the first feature that catches your attention? It may be the dining room table, or a picture on the wall. Continue making mental notes (pegs) of specific items in the room. Each one will be a "memory slot" that you'll later use to store information.

3. Imprint the Palace on your Mind

For the technique to work, the most important thing is to have the place or route 100% imprinted in your mind. Do whatever is necessary to commit it to memory. If you're a visual kind of person, you probably won't have trouble with this. Otherwise, here are some tips that help:

> Physically walk through the route, repeating out loud the distinctive features as you see them.
>
> Write down the selected features on a piece of paper and mentally walk through them, repeating them out loud.
>
> Always look at the features from the same point of view.
>
> Be aware that visualization is a skill. If you're having trouble doing this, you may want to develop your visualization skills first.

When you believe you've got your route down pat, go over your route one more time. It's really important to over learn your path through your Memory Palace.

Once you're confident the route is stamped on your mind, you're set. Now you have your Palace. You can use the route repeatedly to memorize just about anything you want.

4. Associate

Now that you're the master of your Palace, it's time to put that authority to good use.

Like most memory enhancement systems, the technique uses visual associations. The process is simple: take a known image like the front door of your house—your memory peg—and combine it with the element you want to memorize. Each memory peg is a distinctive feature of your journey.

Here's the *"right way"* to do a visual association: *Make it crazy, ridiculous, offensive, unusual, extraordinary, animated, nonsensical—after all, these are the things that get remembered, aren't they? Make the scene so unique that it could never happen in real life. The only rule is: if it's boring, it's wrong.*

Although the technique can be used to memorize tons of information, start with something very simple: use your home journey to memorize a grocery list. Suppose the first item in that list is bacon:

Mentally transport yourself to your Memory Palace. The first feature you see in your mind is the front door. Now, in a ludicrous way, visually combine 'bacon' with the sight of your front door. How about giant fried bacon strips flowing out from

CHAPTER 21 THE MEMORY PALACE

underneath the door and reaching for your legs, just like zombies in those B-movies? Feel the touch of the "bacon hands" on your legs. Imagine the smell of evil bacon.

Is that memorable enough? If it is, move on.

Now open the door and keep walking, following the exact route you previously defined. Look at the next distinctive feature, and associate it with the second item to be memorized.

Suppose the second item is eggs and the second feature of your journey is a picture of your mother-in-law. The process is always the same: Feature the next item in your journey through the house with the item to be remembered. Feature...Item. Feature...Item. Just keep mentally associating images until there are no items left to memorize. What did you do with your mother-in-law and the eggs?

5. Visit Your Palace

At this point, you are done memorizing. Since you're new to the technique, you may need to rehearse a little, repeating the journey at least once in your mind.

If you start from the same point and follow the same route, the memorized items will come to your mind instantly as you look at the journey's features. Go from the beginning to the end of your route, paying attention to the specific points and replaying the scenes in your mind. When you get to the end of your route, turn around and walk in the opposite direction until you get to the starting point.

It's all a matter of developing visualization skills. The more relaxed you are, the easier it will be and the more effective your memorization will be.

Here is a practical example, an 8-digit alarm number. Chunk the number into 4-digit groups, and place each group in a memory palace location.

Use 2418-2220 as the numbers you want to remember. Your home is the Memory Palace:

> Start by associating the first memory palace feature (front door) with 2418. Using the peg word system, convert the numbers to words: 24 = Nero, 18 = Dove. Remember, vowels don't count.
>
> *Arriving at the front door, there is Emperor Nero himself, laughing out loud. He is about to set the whole house on fire, but not with matches or a torch. He has a blowtorch; it's a Dove, a wings-fluttering dove. And it chirps as it spits fire!*
>
> Moving on to the second series of numbers: Associate the second memory palace feature (sofa) with 2220. The peg word conversion: 22 = Nun, 20 = Nose.
>
> *As you close the door behind you, the first thing you see is what looks like a nun chanting and jumping up and down on the sofa. She's facing backwards. Touch her shoulder, she turns around, and she's actually a witch! Seeing her is really scary. Guess what? She has the biggest nose ever! And yuck! On her nose is the biggest zit ever seen (yes, getting disgusting is also a great way to help your memory!).*

CHAPTER 21 THE MEMORY PALACE

This may seem like a lot of work for a number, but in fact, it all happens quite fast in the mind. Recovering a number using the process above should take no more than 4 seconds. If you practice conversion and association regularly, you'll be able to do it much faster and with less effort.

The Memory Palace is extremely effective and fun to learn and use. With just a little experience, Memory Palace lists will stay fresh in your mind for many days or weeks.

You can create as many palaces as you want, and they can be as simple or as elaborate as you wish to make them. Each is a "memory bank," ready to be used to help memorize anything, anytime.

See Addendum 6 for another Memory Palace example. The source for the description in this chapter: Litemind.com.

CHAPTER 22
REMEMBER NAMES AND FACES

Remembering names and faces is very difficult for many of us. In terms of priorities, learning how to remember names and faces may be at the top of your list.

Even in the most cloistered environment, remembering names would be a challenge and modern living complicates the process. From the moment we wake up, we're bombarded with names, facts, and data. One morning's New York Times contains more information than an average adult living in the Middle Ages would have encountered during an entire lifetime.

Why You Forget Names and Faces

Names are difficult to remember because they are a collection of syllables with no obvious connection to the person to whom they're attached. American Indians recognized this problem and assigned names to people when they became adults, based on their most prominent characteristics.

Although most of us started out with good memories, over time, we either learn or develop protective ways not to remember. For example, parents often tell their children not to stare; yet staring is a basic way of imprinting faces into memories.

Some people consciously choose not to remember a name because they perceive the person as a threat. Others forget names because, unconsciously, they wish to repress a bad memory. Usually, if you forget a name, there is a reason, conscious or unconscious.

CHAPTER 22 REMEMBER NAMES AND FACES

Another reason remembering names is troublesome for most of us is because modern society is more informal. In her 1922 book on etiquette, Emily Post devoted 18 separate sections of detailed procedures for making formal introductions. Today, when a guest walks into a home, the host or hostess may rattle off a list of names as the other guests nod in turn. Sometimes the noise or music in the room is so loud that hearing the introductions is impossible.

Why You Should Remember

Some believe remembering names is essential to being a good leader. Sam Walton, founder of Wal-Mart, used to keep printed lists of his store managers, so he could memorize their names. He also asked employees to wear large nametags so he could call them by name.

When someone knows your name, but you don't know his or hers, you're at a disadvantage. Power remains in the hands of the person who knows the most names. Name recollection bestows power, improves morale, and solidifies relationships.

The "FACE" Technique

You can learn to remember names or faces by using the mnemonic device FACE, which stands for "Focus, Ask, Comment, and Employ." The FACE technique works.

Here's how:

> **Focus**–Mentally prepare yourself to remember names. For example, before a meeting or party, review the guest list. Familiarize yourself with the names. If a list is not available, enter the event with a positive attitude. Make as many

new contacts as possible and imagine that all the guests are neighbors, church members, potential clients, new employees or people who can help you advance in your important project.

Ask–Asking questions about a person's name serves two important purposes: it helps to verify the name, and it drives the name into your memory. Ask whether a name is a full name or a nickname or how the person came to have that name. Then simply repeat the name. You don't want to mispronounce "Joanne" as "Joan."

Comment–Make a connection between the name and something with personal meaning to you. For example, if you meet someone named Barbara, you could connect her name with the song "Barbara Ann," or with Barbara Bush or Barbra Streisand.

Employ–Using the name in a conversation is the final step in remembering–but use it casually. Don't include it in every sentence; that would be awkward. If you use the new name once in conversation, a second time when you introduce the new person to someone else and finally when you say goodbye, you will have made enough connections to remember the name.

Performing Introductions

Most people who complain about not remembering names and faces insist they have bad memories. Actually, they have untrained memories. If you're in this category and want to correct this problem, start by becoming more disciplined about how you meet people. Here are some specifics:

Treat introductions formally.
Introduce the most important person first. For example, to introduce your boss to your neighbor, say "Harold, I'd like you to meet my boss, Joe Jones. Joe, this is my neighbor, Harold Simpson."

When making introductions, use phrases like: "I'd like to present..." "I'd like to introduce..." or "I'd like you to meet..." After being introduced, find out a few salient facts about the person and use this information to stimulate conversation. When you introduce others, don't leave virtual strangers together, because that could create an awkward situation.

Become a Great Listener

When you meet people, focus on their faces. Make eye contact and pay attention to what they are saying. Give them your undivided attention. Everyone is busy and can become distracted. Don't. Concentrate on the person in front of you. Say something like, "You and Harold are avid golfers, Joe. What's your handicap these days?" Then, later in the conversation, say, "Harold just won a neighborhood golf tournament. There were some scratch players competing, weren't there Harold?"

Appearance

To make sure you'll be able to concentrate on the people you're talking with, clear away any doubts about your appearance. Take the time you need to make sure you look the way you want to look. Comb your hair and straighten your clothing. If you are thinking about yourself, you will not be able to concentrate on the other people in the room, and you will certainly forget their names.

Some Technical Stuff about Memory

Human memory resides in the hippocampus portion of the brain, which is the gatekeeper between short-term and more permanent memories. The hippocampus receives input from cerebral cortex neurons, which transmit the information. Experiences such as combing your hair, noticing a tree, or feeling a breeze are routine, and the hippocampus screens them out of memory. Memories that are significant activate the neural network. Remarkably, new neural connections appear in different parts of the brain for the same fact or event.

The ability of the human brain to make connections between existing memories and new ones is unique, as is remembering a face or name. Creating a memory that is bizarre, while repeating a name and making an association with it, helps retention. These activities activate new neural pathways, resulting in storing the information in more than one part of the brain.

Facial Recognition

Facial recognition isn't a piece of cake (that's why creating unique images is so important). Its value is demonstrated by the substantial science being applied to the task. Facial biometrics is a computer method for the identification of human beings by three main facial features (eigenfaces):

Distinctiveness identifies individual facial traits that differ from those of the general population.

Robustness looks for traits not susceptible to the passage of time.

Measurability refers to how easily facial characteristics can be identified.

Traditional facial recognition computer systems use algorithms to identify facial features by extracting features from an image of the subject's face. For example, one approach analyzes the relative position, size, and/or shape of the eyes, nose, cheekbones, and jaw. These features are then used to search for other images with matching features.

Dimensional Recognition

A newly emerging trend is three-dimensional face recognition. This technique uses 3D sensors to capture information about the shape of a face. The information is then used to identify distinctive features on the surface of a face, such as the contour of the eye sockets, nose, and chin. Dimensional recognition is not affected by changes in lighting. It can also identify a face from a range of viewing angles, including a profile view.

Skin Texture Analysis

Another emerging trend, called skin texture analysis, uses the visual details of the skin in standard digital or scanned images. The unique lines, patterns, and spots in a person's skin are turned into a mathematical space. Tests have shown that with the addition of skin texture analysis, recognition increases 20 to 25 percent.

A Human Approach

But you and I don't have these slick computer techniques at our disposal. We have to use human approaches to make a person's face give us their name.

When you attach a face to a name, you improve your retention. To improve your memory of faces, start thinking like a photographer, a plastic surgeon, or caricaturist. Notice the person's most prominent facial traits. Then, associate the name creatively with the unique facial trait that has meaning to you.

The "NAME" Technique

Another mnemonic technique (in addition to the FACE one) is called NAME. Name takes advantage of the brain's multiple neuron connections and involves the brain's right and left sides. The mnemonic, "NAME," stands for "Nominate, Articulate, Morph, and Entwine."

Here's how:

Nominate—Choose a person's most prominent physical characteristic (such as large ears or blue eyes).

Articulate —Focus on that feature.

Morph—Change a common name, such as "Sam," into an unusual one like "Samurai," or "Sam I Am." The change will enable you to better remember the name and connect it with the person more easily.

Entwine—Picture the person in an unusual and memorable setting. Essentially, entwining is creating a colorful picture

CHAPTER 22 REMEMBER NAMES AND FACES

of the person, emphasizing the features you deemed memorable.

Never Forget a Face

Faces are easier to remember than names, since most of us have better memories for visual events than for auditory ones. In one study, researchers showed subjects slides of 1,000 faces. Then, they showed the subjects the same slides again, with 100 new faces interspersed among them. The subjects were able to identify which faces were new. If the subjects had been asked to listen to a list of 1,000 names and then to identify 100 new names added to the list, few would have been able to detect the new names.

When All Else Fails

Even after you've learned and practiced these techniques for remembering people's names, you still may forget a name. What should you do?

Never guess. You're better off admitting that you have forgotten someone's name than using the wrong name. You can try reintroducing yourself, in the hope that it will prompt the other person to do the same. In social settings where your spouse is present, ask your spouse to introduce him or herself to the person. Another way might be to ask the other person where the two of you last met so you can establish a social connection.

It will help if you keep a diary of the people you meet, when you met and what was discussed. Update your diaries regularly, since we lose most memories within 24 hours.

Everything so far leads to this: remember names and faces by depending on the face to tell you the name. Create a mental picture for names that have meaning (like Fox or Carpenter).

Some other names don't have a meaning but remind you of something tangible (Hudson might remind you of a river). For names that have no meaning, create a Substitute Word that can be pictured in your mind ("ice cream cone" for Cohen). It's not necessary to substitute all the exact name sounds, just the main sounds or elements.

The three steps involved in remembering names:
   The name
   The face
   Lock the two together

1. Substitute Words come into play in a big way when remembering names. Making up a substitute for a **name** forces you to listen, pay attention, and concentrate. Use the NAME and FACE techniques. *There is absolutely no name you cannot find a substitute word for.*

2. Next, concentrate on a unique **facial feature**.

3. Finally, **lock the name and face together.**

Following is a list of last names and substitute words or phrases. See how it works?

Aarons	an on air, air runs
Abbott	abbot, I bought
Abrams	rams, ape rams
Bailey	bale E
Baldwin	bald one, bald win

CHAPTER 22 REMEMBER NAMES AND FACES

Barnett	bar net
Callahan	call a hand
Cameron	camera on
Campbell	soup, camp bell
Daley	daily, day
Daniels	Dan yells
Dawson	door son
Eaton	eat ton, eatin'
Egan	he can, again
Farber	far bar, far bear
Feldman	fell man
Fleming	flaming, lemming
Garrison	carry son
Gerber	go bare, baby food`
Gibson	vodka, give son
Hamilton	hammer ton
Harrison	hairy son
Heller	hello
Issacs	eye sacks, ice axe
Israel	is real, Star of David
Jacobs	Jacob's ladder
Jerome	chair roam
Johnson	Lyndon, yawn son
Kaiser	guy sore, geyser
Kaufman	cough man
Keegan	key can
Lambert	lamb butt
Lederman	leader man, letter man
Leslie	less lie

McDonald	Mack and Duck (Donald)
Mahoney	my whole knee, my honey
Michaels	Mike calls, Mike kills

Harry Lorayne developed the above list

Coming up with a substitute word doesn't necessarily involve all the sounds in the name; just a sound for the main part. That main part reminder is enough for your mind to fill in the rest of the name.

If you can, develop a standard set of images you can use when a familiar name comes up. Always picture a blacksmith's hammer for Smith, an ice cream cone for Cohen, etc. For names that end in berg, see an iceberg. Of course, there are some names that do not require a substitute word or phrase, like Storm, Bell, Brown, etc.

Here's how:

You've met someone and have come up with a substitute word for the last name. (This was the first step: concentrating on the name.)

The second step involves choosing anything to be their identifying feature (hair, hairline, forehead, eyebrows, eyes, ears, nose, complexion, lips, chin, warts—anything). You want this impression to be what you see when you encounter the person again. The benefit to you is that by concentrating on physical features, the face is being etched into your memory.

Now you've got two of the three requirements: a substitute name and an identifying feature. Getting everything together has required you to concentrate, pay attention, listen, and look.

Here's the third step: link the name and the face's outstanding feature together. Do it in a way that is so ridiculous you'll never forget.

From now on, whenever you meet someone, do the drill:

>Make a **substitute word** for their last name

>Identify an **outstanding facial** characteristic

>**Link the substitute word and feature** together in an image that is funny, strange, ridiculous, enlarged, etc.

First Name

You can add a **first name** to your image, using the same substitution rule you used for the last name. If a **professional title** is important, develop a standard you can use in every instance. Use a gavel for a judge, a stethoscope for a doctor, a sailor's cap for someone in the Navy, etc.

You can expand your image to include a companion, children, place of work, hobbies, and on and on. Once you've started using the system, there's no limit to your combinations.

The Three Steps Name Review

>**Remember the name** by creating a substitute word, if necessary, to give the name meaning. This forces you to listen, pay attention and concentrate.

>**Look at the face** and select its most outstanding feature. Doing so forces you to look at, be interested in, and concentrate on the face.

Associate the substitute name word to the outstanding feature. Link the name and face together with a ridiculous association between your substitute name and the outstanding feature of the face. Be Originally Aware.

If you see that person again, the outstanding feature will conjure up the name. You'll remember.

Developing a fabulous memory will not come naturally. Practice, practice, practice.

Learn the peg words, the mnemonics, the substitutions, the associations, the links, and the little tips. You will have a fantastic memory!

It's not that hard. You can do it!

CHAPTER 23
REMEMBER VERBATIM

Recall, don't repeat.

Have you ever had to memorize a document word by word? It's hard to do. When you memorize by rote (repeating the same thing over and over many, many times), you're not using the lessons of this book. We remember best when we can associate or visualize new material in an unusual way and then link the new information to other images already in our long term memory.

Recalling, not repeating, is the way to store information in our brains.

Repeatedly reading something you want to memorize creates different connections in your brain than the act of recalling. **The recalling experience creates new brain connections; it forces your brain to work for you.**

It's much easier to memorize by practicing recalling. Repeating as a way to memorize is much, much harder. When you practice recalling data it strengthens the same brain pathways that will be activated when you need to remember the information later on.

However, you can't practice recalling the material until the information is at least partially contained in your short term memory. So, start by reading the material a couple of times before you start the recalling experience.

Here's how:

Memorize text utilizing the recall process. The method is based on Mark Shead's article, "How to Memorize Verbatim

Text", in his blog, **productivity501**. Lincoln's Gettysburg Address is the example document.

> "Four score and seven years ago our fathers brought forth on this continent, a new nation, conceived in Liberty, and dedicated to the proposition that all men are created equal.
>
> "Now we are engaged in a great civil war, testing whether that nation, or any nation so conceived and so dedicated, can long endure. We are met on a great battlefield of that war. We have come to dedicate a portion of that field, as a final resting place for those who here gave their lives that that nation might live. It is altogether fitting and proper that we should do this.
>
> "But, in a larger sense, we cannot dedicate—we cannot consecrate—we cannot hallow—this ground. The brave men, living and dead, who struggled here, have consecrated it, far above our poor power to add or detract. The world will little note, nor long remember what we say here, but it can never forget what they did here. It is for us the living, rather, to be dedicated here to the unfinished work which they who fought here have thus far so nobly advanced. It is rather for us to be here dedicated to the great task remaining before us—that from these honored dead we take increased devotion to that cause for which they gave the last full measure of devotion—that we here highly resolve that these dead shall not have died in vain—that this nation, under God, shall have a new birth of freedom and that government of the people, by the people, for the people, shall not perish from the earth."

CHAPTER 23 REMEMBER VERBATIM

Using this 278-word speech as the demonstration article, **the goal is to create a method that will force your brain to practice recalling the speech–even before it is fully memorized.**

Start by getting it into your mind so your brain has it–even if you can't recall it. Here are a few methods that will get the words into your head:

Read through it aloud.

Copy the text by hand.

Read through the text and create a short outline.

Have someone else read it to you.

The objective is to get a general familiarity with the piece and to give your brain just enough information to recall the original text without re-reading the original.
Do this:

1. Start by reading the text out loud two or three times so that you get the general idea of the author's intent. (Use one of the other methods shown above if this one doesn't work for you).

2. Create a document that shows just the first letter of each word of Lincoln's speech. (This example uses Mark Shead's software to do this; two other programs are mentioned at the end of the chapter.) Mark's software strips out everything but the first letter of each word, making a very difficult task really easy!

Here's the Gettysburg Address, showing only one letter from each word:

F s a s y a o f b f o t c, a n n, c i L, a d t t p t a m a c e.

N w a e i a g c w, t w t n, o a n s c a s d, c l e. W a m o a g b-f o t w. W h c t d a p o t f, a a f r p f t w h g t l t t n m l. l i a f a p t w s d t.

B, i a l s, w c n d—w c n c—c n h—t g. T b m, l a d, w s h, h c i, f a o p p t a o d. T w w l n, n l r w w s h, b i c n f w t d h. l i f u t l, r, t b d h t t u w w t w f h h t f s n a. l i r f u t b h d t t g t r b u — t f t h d w t i d t t c f w t g t l f m o d—t w h h r t t d s n h d i v—t t n, u G, s h a n b o f—a t g o t p, b t p, f t p, s n p f t e.

3. Now start practicing recalling. Try to repeat the text just by looking at the first letters of each word.

4. If this "first letter" approach is too difficult, try something easier: cover some words, replace some words with blanks, scramble some words, or show the beginning of each line. All of this will help reinforce the text in your memory until (very soon) you will be able to recall perfectly the whole text just by looking at first letters.

5. Once you can do "first letters," you're almost there. Now say the speech without looking at any helps.

To maintain what you have learned will only take repeating the material once or twice every other day.

This way of learning is similar to when you first started learning to ride a bicycle—it was much easier when you had someone

CHAPTER 23 REMEMBER VERBATIM

beside you to hold you every time you started to lean to one side or the other. In no time at all, you were able to do it on your own.

As you try to recite the speech while looking only at the letters of the text you'll probably get part way into it and get confused. Backup a few letters and look beyond the letter you are struggling with to see if you can figure it out. Remember, you're trying to help your brain find the right connections. If you have to, consult the original text, make a note of what confused you and start over.

This technique is much more productive for memorizing verbatim text than anything else. Your goal is to quickly get the words into your short term memory so you can start practicing the recall process that will move the information into long term memory. This method works.

Note: Here is another program that removes all but the first letter of a word: "Memorizenow.com," It is a little easier to find than Mark's. For the fun of it, also check out "redrubberduck.com."

CHAPTER 24
REMEMBER A SCRIPT

This chapter covers remembering your script if you're in a play. Is it difficult to remember your lines? You bet it is.

Cast members who forget their lines are an annoyance and a burden on other actors. Be a hero and help the cast, director, and yourself: quickly memorize your lines and your cues. Study in a way that appeals to as many senses as you can. By seeing, hearing, feeling, and even smelling your material, you reinforce it in your brain and remember it easier.

There are several ways to reinforce information through your senses. Your best bet is to combine appropriate techniques (for you) from those below.

Highlight your lines so you do not have to look all through your script to find them.

Read the script until you fully understand the plot. Understand your character's intention (what they want).

Understand your character's obstacles (what stands in the way of what they want).

Understand their tactics (what they do to get what they want).

Understand their emotional connection to the whole play (if it's sad, happy, or exciting).

Think of a picture story to go along with your lines (then say your lines as you look at the pictures).

CHAPTER 24 REMEMBER A SCRIPT

Get into character by asking yourself questions about your character. If your blocking (blocking means the physical placement of your character) is to walk upstage carrying a towel, ask yourself why your character would do that. You can also get into character by thinking about why your character acts the way they do. Make up a background story for your character—what happened before the script and what is going to happen afterwards.

Read out loud! Read your lines aloud to yourself.

Break it up. Conquer small parts of your script. It is diffcult to memorize all your lines at once. Add lines one at a time until you have your script memorized.

Write out your lines repeatedly. This gets the lines in your subconscious memory. Be very creative and think of a picture story to go along with your lines.

Practice with a partner. Ask the other person to read your script while you rehearse it to them. Ask them to highlight or circle parts that you skipped or jumbled the words. If you don't have a partner, there are a bunch of App's for your phone that can help you memorize and rehearse your lines. Try the free app, "Line Please."

Record your lines. Get a tape recorder, or record the script onto a CD. You can then play it while driving or exercising, reciting your lines along with the recording. Learn your lines and the other actors' cue lines. It's like learning the lyrics to a song…the more you listen to it, the better you are at "singing" along with the recording.

Tips

When you become tired from rehearsing, relax; it helps your brain work better.

Remember the first and last line of a scene. You can improvise if you know those.

If you have parts of your script that you tend to mess up, highlight them. Then go over them and ask yourself why your character would say or mean that. By adding thought, you are memorizing without realizing it.

Write in pencil the movement and placement of your position in a scene (blocking). Most directors tend to change their mind. Use projection (volume) and inflection (speaking with expression) to your advantage.

Don't spend more than an hour at a time trying to memorize. An hour is typically the limit a human can spend memorizing anything.

Make sure that your lines are on cue (these are the lines other actors need to hear to cue their next line, or the technicians needs to hear to cue lights, sounds, etc.) and are exactly right!

CHAPTER 25
REMEMBER LONG-DIGIT NUMBERS

Remembering phone numbers is not the challenge today that it was earlier in this century. Modern technology has solved the problem of remembering telephone numbers by creating data bases of information about those persons we're interested in. However, there always seems to be a situation where the information we want isn't available. We think we knew it, had it in our phone records or on an index card, but don't. Why can't we remember it?

There is a way. Before cell phones with a directory of names and numbers, there was a time when this method was very, very important. This chapter describes the method that worked back then. You may choose to skip this section, but you shouldn't. You'll have situations develop where you'll want to use the techniques described in this chapter. There is a way to store in your head any numbers you want to recall. (If you need additional help, go back to Chapter 16, "Remember Every Number.")

To remember all-digit phone numbers, start with converting the numbers to letters using the phonetic alphabet number equivalents and free letters to make words.

Say you want to memorize your friend Thomas' phone number, 713-249-3140. Here's how: Phone numbers are already broken down into manageable groups so there's no reason to use the Chunk procedure. (See Chapter 19). The first grouping is the three-digit area code, followed by a three-number group and a four number group.

Convert the phone numbers to phonetic alphabet consonants.

The digit	Alphabetic Representation
0	z, s, soft c
1	t or d
2	n
3	m
4	r
5	L
6	j, sh, ch, soft g
7	k, hard c, hard g
8	f, v, ph
9	b, p
10	t or d and s
	a, e, i, o, u, w, h, y x

For example, 713 converts to cdm (or any other combination of letters available from their cells). Add any of the non-counting letters (a, e, i, o, u, w, h, y or x) and make a word.

Converting numbers to words is not easy, even with the free letters. However, computer software makes it easier. If you're stuck and can't come up with a word, try www.phoneticmnemonic.com Enter the numbers from each group and the computer will give you some suggestions. Following are the results from doing that with your three groups:

  713=Academia, academy
  249=Nearby, unwrap
  3140=Amateurs, matures, mothers, motors

CHAPTER 25 REMEMBER LONG-DIGIT NUMBERS

Choose academy, nearby, and amateurs. Then link the words together into a bizarre story like this:

> Members of the **academy** were **nearby** as the **amateurs** tried in vain to push the sculpture into the river.

The sculpture is of your friend, **Thomas**.

Link Thomas' name to the crazy picture and you've got the scene and his phone number locked forever in your memory.

Whenever you think of Thomas, you see robed professors of the **academy** standing **nearby** as inexperienced student **amateurs** try to push the statue of your friend into the river. Your mind remembers his phone number: 713-249-3140.

CHAPTER 26
REMEMBER LICENSE PLATES

License plates are a memory challenge.

It's difficult to remember license plate numbers and letters when they appear to be a random collection of letters and numbers. And since there's no sequence you can count on, you have to develop your own. Try the following chunking technique (it applies regardless of the plate identification; just separate the letters and numbers in a way you find meaningful).

Assume the plate number is MLR7568. Break the license plate number into three parts: two groups of two characters each and one group of three. ML...R7...568. It's easier to remember small groups than to try to remember an entire letter/number combination at once.

Make an association between each small grouping with something familiar to you. For example, perhaps you would think of the letters "ML" as your cousin's initials or the initials of a famous person you admire, Martin Luther.

For the letter/number group "R7", make a question or statement out of the combination. For example, if you know seven people whose names start with R, you might make a mental picture of all seven people inside your car. Then for the number group, 568, think of a way the numbers might mean something to you. For example, "568" could become "five people born in '68."

Say the combination aloud using your associations so that you get the order of the units into your memory. For example, say, "My license plate is Martin Luther, Ronnie's seven, and five born in 68."

CHAPTER 26 REMEMBER LICENSE PLATES

You can depend on your mind putting it all together.

Another approach to the license: Combine the letters, "MLR" to make the word "Mylar." Make "75"= galley;"68"= chef. The words, "Mylar galley chef" should do something for you. Go to the web site www.phoneticmnemonic.com for lots more suggestions.

Set a timer for an hour's rest and then repeat your associations aloud. Test yourself by asking "What's your license number?" Then say the license number without looking at it. If you cannot remember the plate, repeat the question and response once an hour until you can.

Good luck with this one.

Chapter 27
IN CONCLUSION

The memory systems described in this book all use links of some kind.

Remembering requires creating a link that associates two "things" together in a bizarre way so that it's impossible to visualize one without seeing the other inseparably connected to it. To do so may require substituting the image to make it usable.

Mnemonics is the art of assisting natural memory by using a system of artificial aids (links) to help in the recall of names, dates, facts, and figures. Mnemonics is a technique that aids natural information retention by translating information into a form the human brain can better retain.

The Phonetic mnemonic system associates the digits 0-9 with various consonant sounds which are pegs for memory. These consonant sounds can be combined with vowels to form meaningful words, The peg system is easy to learn and provides both visual and physical links that are memory aids. Use the pegs as a way to remember any list of items.

The "Memory Palace" satisfies the scientific requirement that a unique identifier must be used for each linked list of five to nine items. The concept involves going, in your memory, from one unchangeable place in your home to another. Each easily identified and remembered place becomes the "holder" of a group of five to seven or so items.

Go from place to place. Remember anything.

Chapter 27 IN CONCLUSION

When numbers are converted to phonetic letter consonants and non-counting vowels added, the combination is a linked and bizarre word or sentence easily remembered. Get the original numbers back by dropping the non-counting letters and convert the remaining letters back to numbers.

I hope you will find one of the memory systems to be just what you need. Become proficient in its use; dazzle your friends with your amazing memory!

ADDENDUM 1
OTHER PEG SYSTEMS

Number-Rhyme Pegs and Alphabet Pegs

There are other peg systems in addition to the "Consonant-Number" peg list recommended in this book. Two use digits as their base: "Number-Rhyme;" and "Number-Shape." Two others use the alphabet as their base: "Sound Alikes" and "Concrete Alphas." Don't spend a lot of time with any of the systems described in this addendum unless you decide to use one of these instead of the peg system described in Chapter 18.

Number-Rhyme

With Number-Rhyme peg words, you associate with each number a word that rhymes with that number. Here is a widely used version of the number-rhyme list. The peg is a concrete object whose name rhymes with the number.

One-Sun	Six-Sticks
Two-Shoe	Seven-Heaven
Three-Tree	Eight-Gate
Four-Door	Nine-Wine
Five-Hive	Ten-Hen

The simplest use of the Number-Rhyme Pegs is to memorize a straight list of ten objects. However, this system can be used to memorize much more, including lists of sayings, concepts, technical terms, definitions, vocabulary, steps in a procedure, and so on.

Here's a simple example to show you how this works:

Suppose one day you are visiting your grandmother and she decides to tell you her secret recipe for baking a delicious blueberry pie. The problem is, you don't have a pen or paper with you, so if you want to remember the ingredients you will have to rely on your memory.

She tells you that the pie ingredients are blueberries, lemon juice, flour, sugar, cinnamon, butter, eggs, and milk (eight items). You decide to use the Number-Rhyme Peg Method to remember these until you have time to write them down.

Keep in mind that creating the following associations happen very quickly once you have practiced this memory system a few times.

Begin by associating the first ingredient (blueberries) with the first rhyming peg word (sun). For example, picture clearly in your mind a giant, hot sun shining down brightly on the heads of a group of bright blue bears.

Associate the second ingredient (lemon juice) with the second rhyming peg word (shoe). For example, imagine a yellow shoe full of lemons, and you squishing your foot into the lemons to get the shoe on, turning the lemons into lemon juice.

Associate the third ingredient (flour) with the third rhyming peg word (tree). For example, imagine a brightly colored tree whose trunk and leaves are becoming completely covered and overgrown with your favorite type of flower.

Associate the fourth ingredient (sugar) with the fourth rhyming word (door). For example, imagine a solid brown wooden door slamming shut on a white porcelain sugar bowl, splashing the granulated sugar all over your nice clean carpet.

ADDENDUM 1 OTHER PEG SYSTEMS

Associate the fifth ingredient (cinnamon) with the fifth rhyming word (hive). For example, imagine a swarm of bees flying from the bee hive and stinging your male friend who is sinning - sin a man. (If you think gambling is a sin, imagine him rolling dice or playing cards.)

Think of associations for the rest of the ingredients: six, sticks-butter; seven, heaven-eggs, and eight, gate-milk.

Once you have your list of associations, review them quickly after 1 minute, 5 minutes, and 20 minutes. This will help lock the images and the list of items in your mind. For long-term mental storage, review the list again after 2 hours, then once a day for the next three days. Then once a month after that, depending on how well it seems your mind is retaining the information (which varies from person to person).

If you really worked through this example, you'll be amazed at how well you can recall this list of eight items. Try this now: ask yourself, what is item 7? What is item 2? What is item 5? You should be able to instantly remember and say the ingredient. Try doing that quickly with rote memorization alone!

Following are the rhyming words for numbers 11 through 20:

11. Leaven
12. Shelf
13. Thirsting
14. Courting
15. Lifting
16. Sistine
17. Deafening
18. Waitin
19. Knighting
20. Plenty

Other professionals use different rhyming systems. Here's another example:

1. gun (visualize the first item being fired from a gun).
2. zoo (visualize an association between the second thing and a zoo).
3. tree (visualize the third item growing from a tree).
4. door (visualize the fourth item associated with a door).
5. hive (visualize the fifth item associated with a hive or with bees).
6. bricks (visualize the sixth item associated with bricks).
7. heaven (visualize the seventh item associated with heaven).
8. plate (visualize the eighth item on a plate as if it is food).
9. wine (visualize a wine glass containing the nineth item).
10. hen (visualize the tenth item associated with a chicken).

So, to remember a grocery list of 10 items:

1 Apple: Picture an apple being fired from a **gun**.

2 Butter: picture a **zoo** gorilla stomping up and down on a stick of butter.

3 Razor Blades: Picture a **tree** with razor blades for leaves.

4 Soap: Picture a **door** made from soap.

5 Bread: Picture bees flying from a loaf of bread as if it is a **hive.**

6 Milk: Picture a brick house with milk jugs where the **bricks** should be.

7 Cat food: Picture an open can of cat food with **angel wings and a halo.**

8 Bacon: Picture bacon on a **plate.**

ADDENDUM 1 OTHER PEG SYSTEMS

9 Batteries: Picture a wine glass filled with **batteries**

10 Orange juice: Picture a **hen** being squeezed, and orange juice coming out.

Number-shape

The Number-Shape peg system is similar to the Number-Rhyme system, except that instead of using words that rhyme with the numbers as the pegs, you use the shape of the numbers as pegs.

Here are the shape equivalents for the numbers 1 through 10:
1. Pencil
2. Swan (curvedneck)
3. Love heart
4. Yacht Sail
5. Sea Horse (facing right)
6. Golf Club
7. Cliff Edge
8. Hourglass
9. Balloon on a stick
10. Fork and Plate

To associate an item of information with a number-shape, associate the shape with the information. For example, to associate "tomato" to position number two in the list, associate swan with tomato. Imagine a swan bouncing a bright red tomato up and down on its beak. Then, when you think of "two," it reminds you of "swan," which reminds you of tomato.

Like the other peg systems, the complexity of the information that can be associated with a number can be much greater than simply a tomato or other physical object.

Sound Alikes

This method uses the alphabet instead of numbers, creating a list of 26 letters. The sound-alike alphabet words rhyme with the letter they are associated with:

A	Hay	J	Jay	S	Sass
B	Bee	K	Key	T	Tea
C	See	L	El	U	Ewe
D	Deed	M	Hem	V	Veal
E	Eve	N	Hen	W	Double You
F	Effort	O	Hoe	X	Ax
G	Jeep	P	Pea	Y	Wire
H	Age	Q	Cue	Z	Zebra
I	Eye	R	Oar		

To memorize a list of up to 26 items, you would create for the first item a mental image of "hay" interacting with the first item. For the second item: a "bee" stinging the second item, etc.

Concrete Alphas

In this system, each peg word begins with an alphabet letter (this is the "concrete alpha"—it's set in concrete!). Following is a list of pegs:

ADDENDUM 1 OTHER PEG SYSTEMS

A Ape	J Jack	S Stock
B Boy	K Kite	T Toy
C Cat	L Log	U Umbrella
D Dog	M Man	V Vans
E Egg	N Nut	W Wig
F Fig	O Owl	X X-Ray
G Goat	P Pig	Y Yak
H Hat	Q Quail	Z Zoo
I Ice	R Rock	

The association process is the same as for the other systems.

ADDENDUM 2
PRACTICAL STRATEGIES FOR REMEMBERING

As you become involved in memory issues and techniques, check the following common memory problems and note the ways to overcome them. You may be able to implement these suggestions while developing memory techniques.

What You Forget	How to Remember Better
Names	When you meet someone for the first time, use his or her name in conversation. Think about whether you like the name. Think of people you know well who have the same name. Associate the name with an image, if one comes to mind (for example, link the name Sandy with the image of a beach). Record the person's name in your memory notebook, personal organizer, or address book.
Where you put things	Always put things you use regularly, such as keys and eyeglasses, in the same place. For other objects, repeat aloud where you put them. As you put an object down, make a point of looking at the place where you put it. If you still don't think you'll remember, record in your memory notebook or personal organizer where you put the object.

ADDENDUM 2 PRACTICAL STRATEGIES FOR REMEMBERING

What people tell you	Ask someone to repeat what he or she just said. Ask the person to speak slowly; that way, you'll be able to concentrate better. If the information is lengthy or complicated (such as advice from your doctor), use a small cassette recorder or take notes while the person is talking.
Appointments	Record them in an appointment book, in a calendar that you look at daily, or in your personal organizer.
Things you must do	Record them in your personal organizer or calendar. Ask a friend or relative to remind you Write yourself a note and leave it in a place where you'll see it (for instance, on the kitchen table or by the front door). Leave an object associated with the task you must do in a prominent place at home (for example, if you want to order tickets to a play, leave a newspaper ad for the play near your telephone). If you must do something at a particular time (such as take medicine), set an alarm.

Adapted from Winifred Sachs, Ed. D., Center for Cognitive Remediation and Treatment, Beth Israel Deaconess Medical Center

ADDENDUM 3
MEMORY BOOKS

It seems everybody is writing a book on memory improvement, me included. Here's a listing of some of my favorites.

Aging Memory by John Leslie

Brain Boot Camp by Tony Buzan

Effective Memory Techniques in a Week by Dominic O'Brien

How to Develop a Brilliant Memory Week by Week by Dominic O'Brien

How to Develop a Perfect Memory by Dominic O'Brien

How to Improve Your Memory in Just 30 Days by Ron White

How to Master the Art of Remembering Names by Dean Vaughn

How to Remember Anything: The Proven Total Memory Retention System by Dean Vaughn

Improve Your Memory by Robert Allen

In the Palaces of Memory: How We Build the Worlds Inside Our Heads by George Johnson

Learn to Remember by Dominic O'Brien

Maximize Your Memory by Johnathan Hancock

Maximize Your Memory by Ramón Campayo

Memory from A to Z: Keywords, Concepts, and Beyond by Yadin Dudai

Memory Pack by Andi Bell

ADDENDUM 3 MEMORY BOOKS

Memory Power For Exams by William G. Browning

Memory Power: You Can Develop a Great Memory by Scott Hagwood

Memory, a Very Short Introduction by Jonathan Foster

Mind and Memory Training by Ernest E. Wood

Mind Performance Hacks by Ron Hale-Evans

Mindhacker: 60 Tips, Tricks, and Games to Take Your Mind to the Next Level by Ron Hale Evans and Marty Hale Evans

Moonwalking with Einstein by Joshua Foer

Remember Every Name Every Time by Benjamin Levy

Remember Everything You Want and Manage the Rest: Improve your Memory and Learning, Organize Your Brain, and Effectively Manage Your Knowledge by Helmut Sachs

Remember, Remember by Ed Cooke

Super Memory, Super Student by Harry Lorayne

The Amazing Memory Kit by Dominic O'Brien

The Art of Memory by Frances Yates

The Book of Memory: A Study of Memory in Medieval Culture by Mary Carruthers

The Medieval Craft of Memory by Carruthers and Ziolkowski

The Memory Book by Harry Lorayne and Jerry Lucas

The Memory Palace of Matteo Ricci by Jonathan Spence

The Memory Palace: Learn Anything and Everything by Lewis Smile

The Mind Map Book by Tony Buzan

The Mind of a Mnemonist by A. R. Luria

The Student Survival Guide by Chambers & Colliar

Theories of Memory: A Reader by Rossington and Whitehead

Use Both Sides of Your Brain by Tony Buzan

Use Your Perfect Memory by Tony Buzan

Yellow Elephant by Tansel Ali

You Can Have an Amazing Memory: Learn Life Changing Techniques and Tips from the Memory Maestro by Dominic O'Brien

Your Brain, the Missing Manual by Matthew Mac Donald

Your Memory: How It Works and How to Improve It by Kenneth Higbee

ADDENDUM 4
DON'T WANT TO LEARN ANY MEMORY TECHNIQUES?

If learning the memory techniques of professionals proves to be more than you want to do, there are other things to do that will help you think faster, improve recall, comprehend information better, and unleash your brain's potential.

Here's a list of over 100 items that will boost your brain power:

1. Deliver more than what's expected.
2. Solve puzzles and brainteasers.
3. Cultivate ambidexterity. Use your non-dominant hand to brush your teeth, comb your hair or use the computer mouse. Write with both hands simultaneously. Switch hands for knife and fork.
4. Embrace ambiguity. Learn to enjoy things like paradoxes and optical illusions.
5. Learn mind mapping. (OK, this is a technique.)
6. Block one or more senses. Eat blindfolded, wear earplugs, shower with your eyes closed.
7. Develop comparative tasting. Learn to taste wine properly, or chocolate, beer, cheese, or anything else.
8. Find intersections between seemingly unrelated topics.
9. Learn to use different keyboard layouts. Try Colemak or Dvorak for a full mind twist!
10. Scamper ("scamper" is a mnemonic that stands for: substitute, combine, adapt, modify, put to another use, eliminate, reverse).
11. Turn pictures or the desktop wallpaper upside down.
12. Become a critical thinker. Learn to spot common fallacies.

13. Learn logic. Solve logic puzzles.
14. Get familiar with the scientific method.
15. Draw. Doodle. You don't need to be an artist.
16. Think positive.
17. Engage in arts—sculpt, paint, play music—or any other artistic endeavor.
18. Learn to juggle.
19. Eat 'brain foods'.
20. Be slightly hungry.
21. Exercise!
22. Sit up straight.
23. Drink lots of water.
24. Deep breathe.
25. Laugh!
26. Vary activities. Get a hobby.
27. Sleep well.
28. Power nap.
29. Listen to music.
30. Conquer procrastination.
31. Go technology-less.
32. Look for brain resources in the web.
33. Change clothes. Go barefoot.
34. Master self-talk.
35. Simplify!
36. Play chess or other board games. Play via the Internet (particularly interesting is to play an ongoing game by e-mail).
37. Play 'brain' games like Sudoku, crossword puzzles or countless others.

Addendum 4 DON'T WANT TO LEARN ANY MEMORY TECHNIQUES?

38. Be childish!
39. Play video games.
40. Be humorous! Write or create jokes.
41. Create a List of 100 'anythings'.
42. Have an Idea Quota.
43. Capture every idea. Keep an idea bank.
44. Incubate ideas. Let ideas percolate. Return to them at regular intervals.
45. Engage in 'theme observation'. Try to spot the color red as many times as possible in a day. Find cars of a particular make. Invent a theme and focus on it.
46. Keep a journal.
47. Learn a foreign language.
48. Eat at different restaurants–ethnic restaurants specially.
49. Learn how to program a computer.
50. Spell long words backwards. !gnignellahC
51. Change your environment. Change the placement of objects or furniture, or go somewhere else.
52. Write! Write a story, poetry, start a blog.
53. Learn sign language.
54. Learn a musical instrument.
55. Visit a museum.
56. Study how the brain works.
57. Learn to speed read.
58. Find out your learning style.
59. Dump the calendar!
60. Try to mentally estimate the passage of time.
61. "Guesstimate". Are there more leaves in the Amazon rainforest or neuron connections in your brain?

62. Make friends with math. Fight 'innumeracy'.
63. Build a Memory Palace.
64. Learn a peg system for memory.
65. Have sex! (Sorry, no links for this one!)
66. Memorize people's names.
67. Meditate. Cultivate mindfulness and an empty mind.
68. Watch movies from different genres.
69. Turn off the TV.
70. Improve your concentration.
71. Get in touch with nature.
72. Do mental math.
73. Have a half-speed day.
74. Change the speed of certain activities. Go either super-slow or super-fast deliberately.
75. Do one thing at a time.
76. Be aware of cognitive biases.
77. Put yourself in someone else's shoes. How would different people think or solve your problems? How would a fool tackle it?
78. Adopt an attitude of contemplation.
79. Take time for solitude and relaxation.
80. Commit yourself to lifelong learning.
81. Travel abroad. Learn about different lifestyles.
82. Adopt a genius. (Leonardo is excellent company!)
83. Have a network of supportive friends.
84. Get competitive.
85. Don't stick with only like-minded people. Have people around that disagree with you.
86. Brainstorm!

Addendum 4 DON'T WANT TO LEARN ANY MEMORY TECHNIQUES?

87. Change your perspective. Short/long-term, individual/collective.
88. Go to the root of the problems.
89. Collect quotes.
90. Change the media you're working with. Use paper instead of the computer; voice recording instead of writing.
91. Read the classics.
92. Reading effectively is a skill. Master it.
93. Summarize books.
94. Develop self-awareness.
95. Say your problems out loud.
96. Describe one experience in painstaking detail.
97. Learn Braille. You can start learning the floor numbers while going up or down the elevator.
98. Buy a piece of art that disturbs you. Stimulate your senses in thought-provoking ways.
99. Try different perfumes and scents.
100. Mix your senses. How much does the color pink weigh? How does lavender scent sound?
101. Debate! Defend an argument. Try taking the opposite side, too.
102. Use time boxing.
103. Allocate time for brain development.
104. Have your own mental sanctuary.
105. Be curious!
106. Challenge yourself.
107. Develop your visualzation skills. Use it at least 5 minutes a day.

108. Take notes of your dreams. Keep a notebook by your bedside and record your dreams first thing in the morning or as you wake up from them.
109. Learn to lucid dream.
110. Keep a lexicon of interesting words. Invent your own words.
111. Find metaphors. Connect abstract and specific concepts.
112. Manage stress.
113. Get random input. Write about a random word in a magazine. Read random sites using StumbleUpon or Wikipedia.
114. Take different routes each day. Change the streets you follow to work, jog or go back home.
115. Install a different operating system on your computer.
116. Improve your vocabulary.
117. Go beyond the first "right" answer.
118. Reverse your assumptions.
119. Transpose reality. Ask "What if?" questions.
120. Find novel uses for common objects. How many different uses can you find for a nail? 10? 100?
121. Learn creativity techniques.

Note: The webpages, "litemind," "omharmonics," and" 99u" were the primary sources for these suggestions.

ADDENDUM 5
SOME MORE GREAT AND EASY WAYS TO ENHANCE YOUR EVERYDAY MEMORY

Get Organized

Organization is one of the bedrock concepts for improving everyday memory performance. Being organized is a matter of creating effective systems for routinely handling different types of information and everyday situations that require memory. Once an organizational system is in place and running smoothly, you can be assured the information the system has been set up to handle will be available. Once established, time you would otherwise have spent looking for the data or the thing you have control over, you can spend your freed-up time doing other things.

Manage Low-Contrast Information

Most people need to mentally access a multitude of pieces of information throughout the day. There's an awfully lot information assembled by your mind. You probably don't give much thought to it until you need it and don't know where it is.

The human brain was not particularly well designed to lug around all of these pieces of information in a way that makes them easily accessible. Think of telephone numbers, birthdays, anniversaries, historical dates, etc.

There is an easy way to handle this segment of your life and it doesn't require a memory system you carry around in your head. According to Wikipedia, the first modern attempt to store information was a personal digital assistant (PDA). It was a mobile device that functioned as a personal information manager. Wonderful in its beginning (1984), PDAs are now considered obsolete with the widespread adoption of smartphones.

What's your cousin's phone number? When is your aunt's birthday and what is her favorite wine? Time-honored organizational tools like the address book, desk calendar, note pad, and to-do list, morphed into a single, compact, portable device. PDAs are great for entering recurring events, such as your aunt's birthday and her favorite wine.

You can link contact data to appointments, organize time-sensitive to-do lists, and take paperless notes. Modern devices do wonderful things for us, and they continue to get smarter and smarter! But the old-fashioned pen-and-paper method can also be effective for helping you remember everyday details. Whichever tool you select, high-tech or low-tech, the key is utilizing it consistently to record and organize your daily flow of information.

Meetings and Appointments

Record your appointments and important dates in your phone and keep it with you at all times. If you don't use a smart phone, use a notebook-style weekly calendar that has a page for writing down important information. Check in with your phone or appointment book regularly.

Daily Tasks

Keep a list of the miscellaneous things that you have to do each day or week, people to call, items you need to purchase, routine maintenance on your car or home, and so on. Check your task list at regular intervals or at least at the start and end of each day.

Names, Addresses, and Phone Numbers

Keep your address book up to date with complete contact information for friends, family, and professionals or companies with whom you do business. If there is something specific you want to remember about a particular person (for example, the names of his or her children), note this within your contact information. If it's been a long time since the two of you were together, referring to the note in your address book can serve as a cue to help sharpen your memory for important personal details.

Vital Information

Keep a written record of vital information like the following:
- Your medical history
- Names and phone numbers of your doctors and health insurance company
- Emergency procedures
- Your homeowner's insurance contact information
- Credit card information
- Medications you take and when to take them
- Work and cell numbers of your closest relatives and friends
- Password protecting sensitive personal and financial information is always a good idea.

Store important documents, such as insurance papers and medical records, in a logically organized and clearly tabbed file cabinet or other designated location (such as your Going Away Book).

Make sure that more than one family member knows where you keep sensitive information, such as passports, wills, original receipts for valuable possessions, and other primary financial information.

Although it's very personal, if you are incapable of accessing it, someone else should be your backup.

Belongings

Create a system for keeping track of personal items. Designate a specific place in your home for your most important personal belongings (keys, cell phone, glasses, wallet, handbag, laptop computer, and so on) and always them there when you're not using them.

Checklists

For procedures that you use infrequently and may have trouble remembering (for example, using a digital camera, burning a CD, setting the alarm clock or the thermostat) write the steps down and keep them with the relevant equipment and product manuals. If you can, create a backup file in your computer.

Destinations

Keep maps of your area and other places you visit regularly in your car (MapQuest is a great service). You can also store locations in your auto's GPS system. Organizations like AAA also provide maps and information. Before going somewhere new or unfamiliar, locate your destination and route on a map or use one of the other methods.

Maintain a Clutter-Free Environment

Keeping your personal and workspaces uncluttered induces you to create systems for storage, which in turn helps you remember where things are. Minimizing clutter will minimize distraction and allow you to focus more intensively on what's in front of you, increasing the likelihood that you will absorb and retain new information. (Sounds easy?)

Staying focused and insuring understanding

If remembering is a priority, staying focused is really important. There are ways to improve your ability to learn new information that you hear, read, and see and then commit it to memory. Don't give up. Improve your focus, increasing the likelihood of absorbing and remembering information. This book will be a big help!

Focus

Staying focused and absorbing dense information at a high rate of speed becomes more difficult with age. One cognitive aging theory is that a slowdown in the speed of information processing is the fundamental cause of age-related memory loss. Reduced processing capacity creates an informational bottleneck; the result is that less information passes from working memory to short-term storage.

When someone is talking to you, look at the person and listen closely. If you did not understand something that was said, don't be shy about asking the person to repeat it to speak more slowly. Confidence in knowing will more than offset the embarrassment you may experience at the moment. The same applies to absorbing written material: reading a difficult passage a second time to ensure comprehension is usually preferable to forging ahead with partial information.

If the information you are hearing is something you need to keep in mind in order to do something later, paraphrase what was said or incorporate it in a response. For example, if your friend says, "We can go to the little Italian restaurant on Main Street or the fast food joint on Broadway." You might ask, "Which do you prefer, Italian, or fast food?"

Minimize interruptions

If someone asks you something while you're in the middle of reading or working, ask if the person can wait until you're finished. Don't answer the phone until you've completed what you're doing; let your voice mail or answering machine take the call.

Repeat

Repetition helps you encode information by forcing you to pay attention to it. To more effectively remember factual information, repeat it, either out loud or to yourself. When you meet someone for the first time, try repeating the person's name during the introduction. Then, as the two of you exchange information, use the back and forth flow of data as an opportunity to insert their name into the conversation. Repeat their name as often as practical.

Ensure Comprehension

Understanding something is a prerequisite for remembering it. When you grasp a difficult concept or the internal logic of a complex mathematical system, you have a leg up in remembering all of the associated minutiae that go along with it. Comprehension allows you to appreciate similarities between new material and old material. Associating something new to something familiar enhances memory. Asking questions is one way to check comprehension. Repeating newly learned material to another person induces you to organize it in your own thinking; teaching someone else a new concept forces you to become entirely comfortable and fluent with it yourself. Use a memory device like linking to tie new data together.

Make a Note

In addition to writing down or recording addresses, phone numbers, and other information that you need on a regular basis, write down important things you need to know even just once or occasionally. We all have had the experience of having an important thought spontaneously come to mind while we're in the midst of an activity. Perhaps you're driving to town and a new idea occurs to you. Or it could be a question you want to ask your doctor at your next checkup, an idea for your daughter's birthday present, a book you'd like to read, or restaurants you'd like to try. Don't assume you will be able to recall the thought 30 minutes later when you're sitting at your desk; make a note as soon as you can. The purpose isn't simply to have a written or oral reminder. The act of writing something down or speaking it aloud helps reinforce it in your memory: so-much so that you might not need to refer to your notes to cue your recall.

Practice Spaced Rehearsal

Although you might assume that intensive exposure to new information (cramming) is the best way to learn something, research has taught us that this is not the case. Learning that is spread out over time (spaced rehearsal) is more durable than learning that is concentrated within a short period (massed trials). You will remember something more effectively if you rehearse it once a day for three days than if you rehearse it ten times in ten minutes.

Do the Little Things Now

Don't clog up your to-do list with little tasks that can be dispatched quickly. When you receive a small request that requires a response, the time it takes to file it for future action plus the time you will spend getting back up to speed on it for a second time ends up being time wasted. Dispensing with a little job right away obviates the need to remember it later.

Be Patient

One of the main reasons memory capacity declines with age is that the brain processes information more slowly. But just because it takes longer to absorb something doesn't mean that you won't get it eventually. Give yourself time to understand new information.

One of the findings of a MacArthur Foundation study was that many of the participants said that mental pursuits were important. They could compensate for the slower brain processing by being patient with themselves and working harder. There's a lesson here for the rest of us: perseverance helps keep the mind sharp.

Repeat Things

Saying things aloud will strengthen your memory for them. You get feedback by saying them aloud too, which will help you remember the information.

Envision the information

If you can imagine what the item is that you are trying to remember, you're likely to retain it. Visual images are the easiest type of information to remember.

Create an association

Associate the information you're trying to remember with something that's familiar to you. For example, if you've met someone new who looks like a friend from school, try linking the new person's name with your friend's name. This is a great memory technique.

Become emotionally involved

You can improve your memory of information if you create a funny or unusual association.

Sleep on it

We often solidify memories overnight. Give yourself some time to develop recall for new information.

Limit size

It's easier to remember small chunks of information, so memorize small pieces of information at a time.

Take the stairs

Exercise benefits your head as much as the rest of your body. Overall, cardiorespiratory fitness also lowers the risk of obesity, diabetes, and cardiovascular problems—all known risk factors for Alzheimer's disease. Theories on why that's so range from improved blood flow to the brain to less brain shrinkage.

Experts recommend making regular aerobic workouts part of your routine. Failing that, it appears that even small efforts add up. So avoid elevators. Park at the far end of the parking lot. Start by walking around your block in the evenings, and add a few minutes more each day.

Change your computer screen wallpaper

When doing routine things, the brain runs on autopilot. Novelty, on the other hand, literally fires up the brain as new data creates and works new neural pathways. Shake up what you see and do every day: if your computer screen background is "invisible" to you, run a program that mixes it up every day or every hour.

Steal some zzz's by daylight

It's while you're sleeping that your brain sorts, consolidates, and stores memories accumulated during the day—that's why eight hours at night is so valuable. But a mere six-minute nap is as valuable as a full night's sleep to short-term recall, according to German research. And a 90-minute nap has been shown to speed up the process that helps the brain consolidate long-term memories.

Take a mental "photograph"

ADDENDUM 5 SOME MORE GREAT EASY WAYS TO ENHANCE YOUR EVERYDAY MEMORY

Memories aren't just stored in one spot in the brain; bits of data are processed and stored in different areas. To help make the memory of an incident last, take a "snapshot" of it while you're in the moment, using all your senses. Look around and think about what you see. Notice colors and textures. What do you smell? If you're eating, drinking, or kissing, what's the taste? This "mental camera" trick can help you hang onto a happy memory longer. But it can also help you remember where you parked your car.

Eat less

After only 12 weeks, healthy volunteers (average age 60) who reduced their daily calories by 30 percent scored 20 percent better on memory tests, University of Munster (Germany) researchers reported. The possible reason: decreased levels of insulin, created when the body processes food, and of the inflammation-associated molecule C-reactive protein. Both factors are linked to improved memory function.

The people in the study were cautioned to consume not less than 1,200 calories a day. If cutting back on your diet by nearly a third seems too daunting, focus on eating less fat, meat, and dairy products. Columbia University Medical Center researchers reported that in a long-term study of than 1,300 participants, those with the highest adherence to a Mediterranean diet rich in vegetables, legumes, fish, and monounsaturated oils (like olive oil) but low in fat, beef, and dairy had the lowest risk of developing mild cognitive impairment and Alzheimer's disease.

Try a "brain-training' game or join a "brain gym"

The science is promising, if not conclusive, as to whether so-called brain-fitness software can actually improve memory. A 2009 study in the Journal of the American Geriatric Society shows that people over 65 who used a computerized cognitive training program for an hour a day, over a period of eight weeks, improved memory and attention more than a control group. "*Luminosity*" is a program available on the web.

Spend some time online

Neuroscientist Gary Small, director of the UCLA Memory and Aging Center and author of "Brain," says searching the Web is a bit like using a brain-training course. His researchers used MRI to measure brain activity in Web users ages 55 to 76. The net-savvy users showed twice as much brain activity, especially regarding decision-making.

Stop and sip a cuppa

Green and black teas have a protective effect on memory, possibly by influencing enzymes in the brain. Caffeine sparks concentration, too. And Finnish and French researchers say people who drink moderate amounts of coffee at midlife (as many as three to five cups daily) have lower odds of developing dementia in late life.

Another benefit: Taking a coffee or tea break(s) in your day is a good opportunity for de-stressing.

See a doctor if you feel depressed

Maybe it's "just a mood," but untreated depression is common and can impair memory. Talk therapy and/or antidepressant medication can resolve the problem. Two red flags worth mentioning to a physician: a loss of interest in things that once gave you pleasure and a persistent sense of hopelessness.

People at higher risk for depression include caregivers of older people and those who have a family history of depression.

Take the "multi" out of your tasking

Especially when trying to learn something new, people remember less well if they were multitasking while learning, UCLA researchers have shown. If, for example, you're studying while listening to the radio, your memory recall may be dependent on the music to help retrieve the information later. Replicating the same circumstances is difficult. Try to learn something new when you can give it your full concentration. Cut out distractions like the TV in the background or pausing every few seconds when you hear the "ding" of your e-mail or text-message inbox.

Keep your blood sugar under control

If you're diabetes-free, work to maintain a normal weight and follow a balanced diet to reduce your odds of developing the disease. If you're a type 2 diabetic already, follow medical advice for managing blood sugar levels.
New research shows that brain functioning subtly slows as diabetics' blood sugar rises and the blood vessels that supply the brain are damaged. This process begins well before memory problems become obvious, or even before there's a diabetes

diagnosis.

Waggle your eyes back and forth

To help you remember something important, scan your eyes from side to side for 30 seconds. This little exercise helps unite the two hemispheres of the brain, say researchers at Manchester Metropolitan University in England. When the two hemispheres communicate well, you're better able to retrieve certain types of memories.

Eat your green vegetables

There's no such thing as an "anti-Alzheimer's diet." But people who are deficient in foliate and vitamin B^{12} have an increased risk of developing dementia. (In comparison, the research is iffy on the benefits of taking so-called memory enhancers: vitamin C supplements, ginkgo biloba, and vitamin E.)

Great vegetable sources of foliate include romaine lettuce, spinach, asparagus, turnip greens, mustard greens, parsley, collards, broccoli, cauliflower, and beets. For vegetable haters, the nutrient is also abundant in lentils, calf's liver, pinto beans, and black beans.

Don't ignore sleep apnea

People with sleep apnea, a condition involving blocked airways that causes people to briefly stop breathing during sleep, show declines in brain tissue that stores memory, researchers at UCLA reported.

More than 12 million Americans have obstructive sleep apnea. If your doctor has suggested you have the condition, be vigilant about trying treatments such as wearing oral appliances and masks, losing weight, and surgery.

Learn something new that's a real departure for you

If you're a Sudoku fan, you might think a good way to stretch your mind would be to take up a different Japanese numbers game, like Kenken or Kakuro. But an even better strategy for a nimble brain is to pursue a new kind of activity using skills far different from those you're accustomed to using.

If you ordinarily like numbers, try learning a language. If you're an ace gardener, try painting flowers instead.

Quit smoking cigarettes

The relationship between smoking and Alzheimer's disease is hazy. But smokers do develop the disease six to seven years earlier than nonsmokers.

Eat some chocolate!

Every year some study extols the virtue of dark chocolate. The effects of this wonder-food (or, at least, wonderful food) on memory have not gone ignored by researchers. In 2007, a Journal of Neuroscience study reported on the memory-boosting effects in rats of a plant compound called epicatechin, possibly because it fueled blood vessel growth. In addition to cocoa, epicatechin is found in blueberries, grapes, and tea.

Put everything in its place

While novelty is like growth hormone to the brain, your memory needs a certain amount of familiarity to keep your life functioning smoothly. Place your keys and glasses in the same place all the time. Write notes to yourself as reminders (the very act of writing will help your recall). If you want to remember your umbrella tomorrow morning, place it right at the door, so you won't miss it.

Don't retire

Good news for those who can no longer afford to quit: Provided you like your work, you're helping your brain by sticking with it as long as you can. A satisfying work life offers social stimulation and decision-making opportunities--and exercises problem-solving skills.

Next best: Volunteering, such as at a school or museum, where your training involves learning new material and the task involves interacting with others.

Throw a party

Being around other people lowers one's risk of developing dementia. The catch: They should be people you enjoy, who make you feel engaged and stimulated. People who are physically isolated (not around people) or emotionally isolated (around people but feeling lonely nevertheless) are at higher risk for depression.

Just go easy on the alcohol at those parties. Studies on its effect on memory are mixed. Long-term, excessive drinking is clearly linked with dementia. Binge drinking also impairs short-term memory. On the other hand, for people who drink moderately (one drink a day), alcohol may have a protective effect.

One study found that in people with mild cognitive impairment (mild memory loss that doesn't necessarily advance to dementia), those who drink less than one drink a day progressed to dementia at a rate 85 percent slower than teetotalers who didn't drink at all.

Get A GPS system

Remembering routes can be challenging, especially if they're not frequent destinations. And following written directions can be difficult for someone with early dementia, or anyone who doesn't want to be a distracted driver. Simple solution: a global positioning (GPS) navigation system in the car. Prices have been dropping since these gizmos were first introduced. Many drivers find it easier to follow verbal instructions than to have to read them. And if you make a mistake, the GPS autocorrects and redirects you.

Medication reminders

Medication management is the bane of both caregivers and relatively healthy adults looking after themselves. Fortunately, a variety of tools exist to help you remember to dispense, or take, meds on time.

Medical alarms can be programmed to send you an e-mail message or a beep to a special watch. Some pill containers themselves will send visual messages

A small portable notebook

Not all memory aids are high-tech, as was mentioned earlier. The lowly notebook can be a lifesaver when it comes to remembering names, details, and to-do lists. The trick is to have the notebook handy at all times. Very small books that slip into a pocket or purse work well.

Train yourself to write down everything you don't want to slip away, like the names of those present at a meeting, the sudden thought to call for a haircut appointment, items to pick up at the grocery store on your way home. The act of writing it down helps to secure a thought in your mind and if you forget, you can look it up.

Create a "don't-lose" basket or shelf. This idea amps up the old adage about "a place for everything." Dedicate a single basket or box to all key items that are often misplaced: car keys, house keys, reading glasses, sunglasses, medications, and anything else used regularly—even cell phones, TV remotes, and sweaters. (Note: For someone with dementia, you'd want to store medications out of sight and out of reach to avoid accidental overdosing.)

A centralized household calendar

It's hard enough to remember your own priorities, let alone everyone else's. Whether your household contains five people and three generations or just one person and a pet, post an oversized calendar in a central place (such as the kitchen).

Use a different colored marker to write down each family member's appointments, invitations, and travels (or, for a pet, dates with the vet or groomer).

Get in the habit of looking at the calendar every morning and consulting it before you make new appointments. Electronic calendars work well for many people, but for others, they're "out of sight, out of mind." A large planner in your line of vision every day is harder to ignore.

Some of this chapter's material is from Achieving Optimal Memory, by Aaron P. Nelson and The Harvard Medical School Guide To Achieving Optimal Memory. Some of the suggestions were described by Paula Spencer Scott, Caring.com senior editor. Other suggestions came from my notes and I didn't record the source.

ADDENDUM 6
A MEMORY PALACE JOURNEY

A most useful and widely used memory aid is the Memory *Palace,* a place or series of places in your mind where you can store information you need to remember in sequence. The palace memory method was described in detail in Chapter 21.

By example, this addendum illustrates how a person would go through the rooms of their home and identify various objects that would be associated with the room and serve as memory pegs. Then, as you developed the various parts of your speech (which you have named, "Home Owners' Dilemma"), you would go to the first location in your palace (the living room) and begin associating points of your speech to peg items in the room.

Your Memory Palace journey moves through the house in this order:
- Living room
- Dining room
- Kitchen
- Office
- Master bedroom
- Bathroom
- Second bedroom

Each room is a part of a linked journey. The listed items within each room are pegs to link specific items relating to your speech.

Although there are many pegs you can use (each room is filled with many pieces of furniture and art), it's best to use not more than five items (pegs) in each room. In a pinch, use ten, but don't unless it's absolutely necessary.

The Living Room Pegs

The living room windows have six wrought iron bars over each of the windows that face the street

Furniture includes a brown chaise lounge, a hickory coffee table, and two Queen Victoria chairs.

The table is lined with bronze, and a tea platter sets upon it.

Two books, one on the American Civil War and the other, a book on the transformation of ladies' fashion in France, are stacked next to the platter.

A plate holds a large chunk of brie cheese and wheat crackers.

A fireplace crackles in the corner with several candlesticks lining the mantle

A large portrait of great-grandfather Robert E. Traill hangs above the fireplace.

A giant chest overflowing with gold coins is tucked between the chaise lounge and the wall.

A snake with an apple in its mouth is coiled around a chair leg.

An ornate little elephant carved out of wood is perched between the candles on the mantel

A tree frog made of quartz is next to the elephant.

The Dining Room Pegs

The dining room mahogany floors are glossy.

The walls are paneled wallpaper, colored purple, green, and gold (the colors of Mardi Gras).

The dining room table is white, rectangular, and marble with gold.

The eight chairs surrounding the table are colored mauve made of steel.

A Leonardo da Vinci painting is hanging on the wall at the head of the table; a painting of the Horn of Africa hangs on the wall alongside it.

A swan is nesting in the chandelier with feathers floating down onto the table

The Kitchen Pegs

The kitchen has a classic 1940s stove.

A pan is over the fire, and liver is cooking in an inch of butter.

A bunch of Azaleas (state flower of Georgia) are stuffed into a glass vase.

A magazine on Fortune 500 companies sits by a cutting board near the sink.

The tap is running and the drain is clogged, so water is over flowing and gushing onto the ground.

Pinned to the door by a large deadbolt and padlock is a shirt with a triangle painted on it.

The Office Pegs

The office has a drafting table with geology notes strewn across it. Resting on the notes is a snow globe paperweight

A charm bracelet with crosses and clovers rests on the desk.

A black ring made of bone is on the desk.

A mug of beer has been spilled on the floor.

A tall top hat hangs on a hat rack.

A child has decorated the windows with light blue plastic snowflakes.

A leopard skin lays on the floor like a rug.

A framed photograph of Charles Darwin hangs between two windows.

The Master Bedroom Pegs

The master bedroom bed is covered with a heart printed comforter.

Across from the bed is a giant white armoire.
A copy of the New York Times and a tube of red lipstick are set on a vanity table.

A bottle of Glenlivet whiskey is on the nightstand next to a Rolex watch.

A large panda sits alone in bed while watching National Geographic on TV.

A pair of dirty work boots sit under the desk next to a hammer.

The Bathroom Pegs

A claw foot tub in the bathroom is collecting rain water from a leak in the roof.

A stained glass lamp hangs from the ceiling. Lavender oil sits by the tub.

The wall is painted with a red cross in a white field.

A monkey in a yellow hat plays in the water.

The floor is a bright glowing orange color.

The Second Bedroom Pegs

The second bedroom has bunk beds covered with vines that stretch across the ceiling and walls. .

A wind-up toy car drives into the wall repeatedly.

A little boy is perusing Webster's dictionary.

The window blinds are made of licorice

The dresser drawers are pulled out like stairs.

A little girl sits on the top bunk eating cotton candy. Next to her is a husky dog.

Putting It Together

For instance, in the living room you had previously identified the wrought iron bars over the windows as the first peg. To do this you have a mind picture of a room suspended in space and held together by iron bars. Associate your first speech point (the way the houses in the development are isolated from each other by fences) by imagining house after house connected to the other with iron bars which have fires under them and hamburgers roasting on the bars!

Your second living room peg is furniture, especially the two Queen Victoria chairs. Imagine the chairs seated next to the iron bar grills with the elderly Queen Victoria sitting in one of them. She holds in her hand a large black plastic sack, which refers to the second point of your speech (the fences hide the fact that many residents are not taking their garbage to the street on collection days). You have several things to say about that and then remember the portrait of great-grand father Robert E. Traill, hung above the fireplace. That picture includes squirrels, which is your next speech point (the large number of the animals which are breeding quickly because of the food left lying around in so many back yards). This problem would be lessened if trash were taken to the street on collection day.

And on and on….linking four or five of the major speech topics to the various rooms of your house. Remembering would start with the room, followed by your recollection of the room contents, each of which would be associated with the next topic of your speech.

In Summary

In each room of your palace are things that are your pegs to use as memory stops for your speech. As you visit each room, the things you remember become the pegs you associate with your speech topics.

The Memory Palace Journey is based on an article in WikiHow, "How to Do Anything," and on data in Litemind.com/memory-place: "Develop Perfect Memory with the Memory Palace Technique."

ADDENDUM 7
DESCRIPTIVE MNEMONICS

To be the most effective, mnemonics should have at least one descriptive characteristic. The following list (from Wikipedia) is indicative of the many colorful choices available. Just browsing through the descriptive phrases should help when creating a difficult mnemonic. Use as many descriptions as you want.

a bit thick	dubitable
a bit thin	eccentric
abnormal	empty
amusing	excluded
anomalous	extravagant
asinine	fantastic
balmy	farcical
barred	fatuitous
beyond belief	fatuous
bizarre	foolish
childish	freaked out
closed-out	funny
cockamamie	futile
comic	grotesque
contrary to reason	hard of belief
crazy	hard to believe
curious daft	harebrained
disproportionate	high-flown
doubtable	hilarious
doubtful	hollow
droll	hopeless

humorous
idle
illogical
imbecile
imbecilic
implausible
impossible
inane
insane
incoherent
incommensurable
incommensurate
incompatible
inconceivable
incongruous
inconsequent
inconsistent
inconsonant
incredible
irrational
irreconcilable
laughable
logically impossible
loony
ludicrous
mad
meaningless
monstrous
moronic

nonsensical
not deserving belief
not possible
nuts
nutty
odd
oddball
off the wall
open to doubt
open to suspicion
out
out of proportion
outlandish
outrageous
outre
oxymoronic
paradoxical
passing belief
passing strange
peculiar
Pickwickian
Poppycock
potty
preposterous
priceless
problematic
prohibited
quaint
queer

ADDENDUM 7 DESCRIPTIVE MNEMONICS

questionable
quizzical
rich
ridiculous
risible
rubbishy
ruled-out
screaming
self-contradictory
senseless
silly
simple
singular
skimble-skamble
staggering belief
strange
stupid
suspect
suspicious
tall
thick
thin
trashy
twaddling
unbelievable
unconvincing
unearthly
ungodly
unimaginable

unreasonable
unsound
unthinkable
unworthy of belief
vain
wacky
weird
whimsical
wild
witty

ALSO BY JOHN LESLIE

BOOKS

Book of Toasts *
I'm Getting Older, But I'm Not Dead Yet! *
Words… Some Wise… Some Otherwise *
You Died; What Do I Do Now? *
Aging Memory *
Itinerant Preacher
The Home Town Family
Grandmothers
The Scottish Family

LECTURE SERIES

Cowboys, Indians and Presbyterians
Caveman, Rabbit Stew and Jesus
Preparing for the End of Life
Dancing with Doctors

www.ingramcontent.com/pod-product-compliance
Lightning Source LLC
Chambersburg PA
CBHW061255110426
42742CB00012BA/1924